Night of Weeping
and
Morning of Joy

by
Horatius Bonar

Biographical Foreword by
Michael A. G. Haykin

REFORMATION HERITAGE BOOKS
Grand Rapids, Michigan

2008

© 2008 Reformation Heritage Books

Published by
Reformation Heritage Books
2965 Leonard St., NE
Grand Rapids, MI 49525
616-977-0599 / Fax 616-285-3246
e-mail: orders@heritagebooks.org
website: www.heritagebooks.org

Appreciation to Darrin R. Brooker for providing the electronic text.
Visit www.horatiusbonar.com.

Library of Congress Cataloging-in-Publication Data

Bonar, Horatius, 1808-1889.
  Night of weeping ; and, morning of joy / by Horatius Bonar ;
biographical foreword by Michael A. G. Haykin.
      p. cm.
  Contains Horatius Bonar's two classic companion volumes: The night of
weeping and The morning of joy.
  ISBN 978-1-60178-032-4 (pbk. : alk. paper)
  1. Christian life. 2. Suffering--Religious aspects--Christianity. 3.
Joy--Religious aspects--Christianity. I. Bonar, Horatius, 1808-1889.
Morning of joy. II. Title. III. Title: Morning of joy.
  BV4501.3.B657 2008
  248.8'6--dc22
                                                    2007048814

*For additional Reformed literature, both new and used, request a free
book list from Reformation Heritage Books at the above address.*

Table of Contents

Horatius Bonar

Horatius Bonar (1808-1889)

Horatius Bonar was born in Edinburgh on December 19, 1808. His father, James Bonar (1757–1831), was an elder in Lady Glenorchy's Chapel, a bulwark of Edinburgh Evangelicalism that had been founded in 1774 with money donated by Lady Glenorchy (1741–1786), a wealthy patroness of Evangelical causes. However, James Bonar died when Horatius was but thirteen. Thus the greatest influence on him during his early years were his godly mother, Marjory Maitland Bonar (d. 1854), and his eldest brother, James (1801–1867), who, like his father, was an elder at Lady Glenorchy's Chapel and was deeply involved in numerous Evangelical and philanthropic enterprises. There are no known details of Horatius' conversion.

Three influences
Horatius was educated at Edinburgh High School and Edinburgh University before entering the Divinity Hall, where the Professor of Divinity was Thomas Chalmers (1780–1847), whom the Scottish literary figure Thomas Carlyle (1795–1881) once called "the Chief Scottish man of his time." Chalmers had an enormous influence upon the young Bonar; Horatius considered Chalmers the greatest Christian he ever knew.

Another important influence were some lectures on the Book of Revelation that were given in Edinburgh over the years 1828 to 1830 by Edward Irving (1792–1834). At the time, Irving was one of the most popular Presbyterian preachers. In 1833, though, he would be removed from the ministry of the Church of Scotland for espousing erroneous views regarding the humanity of Christ. Horatius Bonar would have agreed with his friend Robert Murray McCheyne (1813–1843) when the latter described Irving as "a holy man in spite of all his delusions and errors." The long-lasting influence of Irving's premillennial convictions on Horatius can be seen, for instance, in *The Quarterly Journal of Prophecy*, a publication that he edited from 1849 to 1873 that was designed to promote premillennial eschatology.

A third important influence upon Horatius Bonar's spiritual growth during his days at the Divinity Hall came from a circle of friends that included three of his brothers, Robert Murray McCheyne, Alexander Neil Somerville (1813–1889), John Milne (1807–1868), and a number of other young men. As the biblical proverb puts it, these men shaped each other as iron sharpens iron (Prov. 27:17).

Leith and Kelso (1833–1866)

After being licensed to preach in 1833, Bonar's first ministerial appointment was at Leith, the port of Edinburgh, where he worked as an assistant minister to James Lewis in the parish of St. John's.

Word of Bonar's effective ministry at Leith spread to a newly established congregation in Kelso, the North Parish Church, which sent a deputation to hear Bonar preach and sound him out regarding a call to their church. Unanimously called to this work on November 30, 1837, Bonar would labor in the Scottish Borders for twenty-nine years.

It was at Kelso that Bonar's gifts as an evangelist blossomed. The keynote that he sounded right from the start of his Kelso ministry was "Ye must be born again" (John 3:7). Bonar was rightly convinced that without this emphasis from the pulpit on the vital need for personal regeneration, "all religion is hollow and superficial."

One of Bonar's successors at Kelso was W. Robertson Nicoll (1851–1923), who was minister there from 1877 to 1885 and later became a well-known author and journalist. Nicoll noted that Bonar's ministry at Kelso was one of "quenchless zeal and unrelenting labor. He set himself to evangelize the Borderland. His name was fragrant in every little village, and at most of the farms. He conducted many meetings in farm kitchens and village schoolrooms, and often preached in the open air."

A writing ministry

Bonar was also convinced of the importance of Christian literature as a vital means of evangelism and Christian nurturing. To that end, he began writing while at Kelso a series of tracts and small booklets that could be printed cheaply and widely distributed. Other authors, including his brother, Andrew (1810–1892), were also involved and the series became known as "The Kelso Tracts." These tracts opened the way for larger literary endeavors.

One of his first books was *The Night of Weeping; or, Words for the Suffering Family of God* (1845). Bonar was well qualified to write *The Night of Weeping* since he and his wife, Jane, had a number of children who did not survive infancy—a fact he alludes to in the pages that follow. *The Morning of Joy*, intended as a sequel to *The Night of Weeping*, was written in the course of 1849 and appeared in print the following year. It, too, was rooted in part in Bonar's experience, for he was in the habit of meditating on the future joys of the church and what would then be her "resurrection-nearness [to] and resurrection-fellowship" with her Lord.

Chalmers Memorial Church, Edinburgh (1866–1889)

Horatius Bonar's final sphere of ministry was in Edinburgh. He received several calls to other spheres of ministry during his time at Kelso but never seriously considered leaving until called in June 1866, to become the first minister at the newly established Chalmers' Memorial Church (now St. Catherine's Argyle Church).

He would be there until his death. The congregation grew significantly under his Spirit-filled preaching, increasing from 61 in October 1866 to 805 in July 1888. He preached up until a year or so before his death in Edinburgh on July 31, 1889.

Bonar's significance

Bonar also wrote a large number of hymns that have rightly led to his being regarded as the finest Scottish hymn-writer of the nineteenth century. His hymns and other literary works, moreover, reveal the rich vitality of nineteenth-century, Scottish Presbyterian piety. As such, they are a marvelous resource for contemporary Evangelicals seeking to know something of their spiritual heritage.

May the two books reprinted in the pages that follow give the reader a taste for other volumes by Bonar and minister to the reader's heart and soul.

Michael A. G. Haykin
Dundas, Ontario
November 27, 2007

The Night of Weeping

Or
Words for the Suffering
Family of God

"Weeping may endure for a night."
— Psalm 30:5

Preface

It is no easy matter to write a book for the family of God. Yet it is for them that these thoughts on chastisement are written. They may be found not unsuitable for the younger brethren of the Man of sorrows. For the way is rough, and the desert blast is keen. Who of them can say aught regarding their prospects here, save that tribulation awaiteth them in every place as they pass along? This they must know and prepare for, grasping more firmly at every step the gracious hand that is leading them on to the kingdom, and looking up for guidance to the loving eye that rests over them with fondest vigilance, ever bright and ever tender, whether in shadow or in sunshine, whether amid the crowds of busy life, or in the solitude of the lonely way.

It is, then, to the members of this family that this little volume is offered. They may find in it something which may not merely interest them, but may also meet their case; something, too, in which, perhaps, they may recognize, not the voice of a stranger, but of a brother: "a companion in tribulation and in the kingdom and patience of Jesus Christ" (Rev. 1:9). For the tones of the suffering brotherhood on earth have something in them too peculiar not to be instinctively recognized. It is said of Arabian airs that they are all plaintive. They all touch some melancholy chord, as if the wail of the desert echo were the keynote of each melody.

It is in some measure thus with the children of the kingdom, while sojourning in this wilderness of earth. "Their voice is ever soft, gentle, and low." Sorrow has smoothed away its harshness, and breathed gentler feeling into its tones. True, it is the voice of gladness, for it is the voice of the forgiven; but still it is sorrowing gladness, calm and serious joy. Their peculiar lot as followers of a hated Lord and their peculiar circumstances, as standing in the midst of a doomed and dying world, have wrought into their spirit a deep though serene solemnity of expression, alike in look and voice. Hence, there is the instinctive recognition among the brotherhood, not only of the family look, but of the family tones. It is of family matters that we speak, and in these each member has a common interest. The "household of faith" has many concerns, and not the least of these are its sorrows. These are the lot of all; and there is no member of the household but has his share in these, either in personal suffering or in helping to bear the burden of others.

What is now written may be found suitable to all, whether actually under chastisement or not. It is, however, presented specially to those who are "in heaviness through manifold temptations," suffering the rebuke of the Lord, passing through fire and through water, with "affliction laid upon their loins" (Ps. 66:11, 12). The bruised reed must not be broken, the smoking flax must not be quenched. The hands which hang down must be lifted up, and the feeble knees confirmed; that which is lame must not be turned out of the way, but rather healed.

Our desire is to minister to the saints in the consolation and admonition of the Lord. We would seek to bear their burdens, to bind up their wounds, and to dry up at least some out of their many tears. To comfort those who mourn is not only to act in obedience to the command, "Bear ye one another's burdens, and so fulfill the law of Christ"; it is to walk by the side of Jesus in His visits of mercy to His suffering saints on earth; nay, it is to be fellow-workers with the Holy Ghost as the church's Comforter in all her tribulations and distresses.

Of these things the world knows little. Its sympathies are not with the saints, either in their sorrow or their joy.

Family concerns, and especially family griefs, are not for strangers to meddle with. They are things too high for them. And how shall they understand them so long as they remain without? They must first come in and take their place among the children beneath the paternal roof. And what should stay them? The gate stands open day and night. They would be welcomed in with the kindliest greetings of love.

But though standing afar off from the saints and unable to mingle its sympathies with theirs, the world still has sorrows of its own, deep and many. To grieve, and yet have no comforter; to be wounded, and yet have no healer; to be weary, and yet know no resting-place—this is the world's hard lot.

Yet it is a self-chosen one. God did not choose it for them. They chose it for themselves. God invites, nay, pleads earnestly with them to quit it, yet they will not. Wretched as it is, they prefer it to the friendship of Him with whom their heart is at enmity, and whose presence is to them all gloom and terror. Yet He continues to entreat them. He does not let them alone. The "many sorrows" which compass them about are His many messages of grace, His unwearied knockings at their fast closed door. He writes "vanity" upon the creature, "weariness and vexation" upon earth's best delights that men may not place their confidence in these. Most mercifully does He hedge them about with disappointment of every form that they may lift their eyes above this earth and beyond these heavens to the enduring blessedness that is at His right hand forever. With what kindness, though with seeming severity, does He mar their best friendships that He may attract them to the communion of His own far better and everlasting companionship? With what compassion does He break in upon their misguided attachments that He may draw them away from earth and bind them to Himself by the more blessed ties of His own far sweeter love? With what tenderness does He tear asunder the bonds of brotherhood and kindred that He may unite them to Himself in far dearer and eternal relationship?

With what mercy does He overthrow their prospects of worldly wealth and bring down their hopes of earthly power and greatness that He may give them the heavenly treasure and make them a "royal priesthood" to Himself in the glorious kingdom of His Son. With what love does He ruin their reputation among men, breaking in pieces their good name which was their idol that He may show them the vanity of human praise, leading them to desire the honor that cometh from God and to know that in His favor is life and that the light of His countenance is the very sunshine of Heaven. Oh, that a weary, brokenhearted world would learn these lessons of grace! Oh, that they would taste and see that God is good! Let them but come home to Him. He will not mock them with shadows, nor feed them with husks. He will satisfy their craving souls; He will turn their midnight into noon; He will give them beauty for ashes, the oil of joy for mourning, the garment of praise for the spirit of heaviness that they may be called trees of righteousness, the planting of the Lord.

Let the world, however, regard God's dealings with them as they may: let not "the children" despise the chastening of the Lord, nor faint when they are rebuked of Him. They at least should know the meaning of His actions toward them, for they know HIM. The world may misunderstand His rebukes or put an unkind construction upon them; they cannot, for they know that "God is love."

The thoughts that follow are designed to assist them in interpreting God's ways, not merely in finding comfort under trial, but in drawing profit from it. I have at least attempted to contribute something toward this end. I have done what I could, rather than what I would. But it may be that the Head of the family will own it, and send it with His own blessing to the scattered members near and far. He knows that they need some such words in season; and that, if thickening signs deceive not, they will ere long need them more. In such a case even this little volume may be helpful. It is written in much weakness, and with many sins to mar it; amid what trials it is of little moment for a stranger to learn. It is written by one who is seeking himself to profit by trial, and trembles lest it should pass by as the wind over the rock, leaving it as hard as ever; by one who would fain in every sorrow draw near to God that he may know Him better, and who is not unwilling to confess that as yet he knows but little.

1

The Family

It was God's purpose from the beginning, not merely to redeem for Himself a people out of a world of sinners, but to bring that people into a peculiar relationship to Himself. It was His purpose to draw them nearer to Himself than any other order of His creatures, and to establish a link of the closest and most peculiar kind between them and the Godhead.

To carry out this purpose was the Word made flesh. "He took not on him the nature of angels; but he took on him the seed of Abraham" (Heb. 2:16). "Forasmuch then as the children are partakers of flesh and blood, he also himself likewise took part of the same" (Heb. 2:14).

Thus a new relationship was established, such as till then could never have been conceived of as even possible. The tie of creation, though not dissolved, was now to be lost in the closer, dearer tie of kindred. "Both he that sanctifieth and they who are sanctified are all of one: for which cause he is not ashamed to call them brethren" (Heb. 2:11). He calls them brethren, and they call Him brother. Being "made of a woman," He has become partaker of our lowly humanity, so as to be bone of our bone, and flesh of our flesh; and we being "born of God" are made partakers of the divine nature, becoming "members of his body, of his flesh, and of his bones." Thus the saints are the nearest kinsman of the Son of God; and if of the Son, then of the Father also, as

He hath said, "I and my Father are one," "believest thou not that I am in the Father, and the Father in me?"

It is thus that the family relationship is formed and God's original design carried out. For thus it is written, "As many as received him, to them gave he power [or the right] to become the sons of God, even to them that believe on his name: which were born, not of blood, nor of the will of the flesh, nor of the will of man, but of God" (John 1:12, 13). And again, "Behold what manner of love the Father hath bestowed upon us, that we should be called the sons of God" (1 John 3:1). We are elevated to creation's highest level. We are brought into the inner circle of the Father's love—nearer His throne, nearer His heart than angels, for we are the Body of Christ, and members in particular—"the fullness of him that filleth all in all."

Out of this new link there springs the family bond between us and the God and Father of our Lord Jesus Christ, "His Father and our Father, His God and our God." And it is especially in this name of family that God delights. He has many names for His redeemed. They are His chosen ones, His people, His flock, His heritage. But it is as His family that He speaks of them oftenest, and it is as such that He bends over them so fondly, as over His first-born—the children of His heart and the desire of His eyes.

But it is needful that we inquire further concerning this family and learn from God's own account of them who and what they are. By nature they are children of wrath, even as others. And thus far there is no original difference between them and the world. But they are the eternally chosen of the Father, "chosen in him [Christ] before the foundation of the world" (Eph. 1:4). This is their true ancestry, and this is their chiefest glory. They are "predestinated...unto the adoption of children by Jesus Christ to himself, according to the good pleasure of his will" (Eph. 1:5). They are quickened together with Christ, from being dead in trespasses and sins, and raised up by the exceeding greatness of God's power, the same mighty power by which He wrought in Christ when He raised him from the dead (Eph. 1:19, 20). They are saved by grace through faith, and that not of themselves, it is the gift of God" (Eph. 2:8). They are reconciled to God by the death of His Son (Rom. 5:10). They are delivered from a present evil world according to the will of God their Father (Gal. 1:4). They are washed in the blood of Jesus and justified by faith in His name. They are redeemed from their vain conversation, not with corruptible things, as silver and gold, but with the precious blood of Christ, as of a lamb without blemish and without spot: who verily was foreordained before the foundation of the world, but was manifest in these last times for them (1 Peter 1:18–20). They are made heirs of God, and joint-heirs with Jesus Christ, kings and priests unto God, who are to reign with Christ forever over a redeemed and restored creation.

Such is the family. Surely they are high born. Their ancestry is from eternity. Their descent is from the King of kings. They are of the blood royal of heaven. And though their present condition be a lowly one, their prospects are the brightest that hope ever painted, brighter than what eye hath seen or ear hath heard. It doth not yet appear what they shall be; but they know that when He shall appear, they shall be like Him, for they shall see Him as He is (1 John 3:2).

But apart from these descriptions which encircle the saved family with such peculiar glory even here, their simple condition of being God's family calls for a little further notice. For it is not outward circumstances that form, or give interest to, a home or a family; it is the living pulse of affection that is beating there. Neither earthly pomp nor earthly poverty can materially alter the real inward character of that little circle of human hearts which man calls a family. Bright skies and sunshine cannot weaken or sever the bond; neither can they allure them away from rejoicing in each other's joy and love.

Dark days and tempests cannot sunder them; they do but make them gather more closely together then, as being all in all to each other. So it is with the family of the redeemed. It is not their outward circumstances or prospects that give them the name; it is something far more tender and deeper than these. It is the pulse of heavenly affection, throbbing through every member and coming down from the infinite heart above; it is this that makes them what they are. It is under this aspect that God delights to look upon them. It is for this reason especially that He has given to them the name they bear.

The word "family" is a sacred one, even among the children of the world. There is a hallowed tenderness about it, which few, save the wickedest, do not feel in some measure. One of their own poets has thus expressed the feeling:

> *Beneath the foulest mother's curse*
> *No living thing can thrive;*
> *A mother is a mother still,*
> *The holiest thing alive.*

I am by no means in accord with the sentiment contained in these words; the language is too strong. Still it shows the world's feeling as to the strength and sacredness of the family bond. And there is much of truth contained, or at least implied, in it. No other earthly circle can be compared with that of the family. It comprises all that a human heart most values and delights in. It is the center where all human affections meet and entwine, the vessel into which they all pour themselves with such joyous freedom. There is no one word which contains in it so many endearing associations and precious remembrances, hidden in the heart like gold. It appeals at once to the very center of man's being—his "heart of hearts." All that is sweet, soothing, tender, and true is wrapped up in that one word. It speaks not of one circle or of one bond, but of many circles and many bonds—all of them near the heart. The family home, the family hearth, the family table, family habits, family voices, family tokens, family salutations, family melodies, family joys and sorrows—what a mine of recollections lies under that one word! Take these away, and earth becomes a mere churchyard of crumbling bones; and man becomes as so many grains of loosened sand, or at best, but as the fragments of a torn flower, which the winds are scattering abroad.

All that is beautiful in human relationship, or tender in human affection, or gentle in human intercourse; all that is lovable and precious in the movements of a human heart from its lowest depth to its uppermost surface—all these are wrapped up in the one word: family. For close-knit bonds, for steadfast faithfulness in love, for depth of sympathy, for endurance in trial and danger—where shall we find anything that can be compared with the story of earth's family circles? Conjugal love, parental love, filial love, brotherly love, sisterly love—all are here. The many streams of human affection empty themselves into it, or flow out of it, for the fertility and gladness of the earth.

We need not wonder, then, that this name should be chosen as one of the church's peculiar names. God delights in it as the name by which His company of chosen ones is to be specially called. The Family of God—that is the church's name. As such He dwells in the midst of it, cares for it, and watches over it. His dealings with it are those of a father— fond yet strict—loving yet wise—sitting among His children, having His eye on each, and ordering in His gracious wisdom all the concerns of His household.

His heart is there! Yes, it is in His church that God's heart may be said specially to be. There it unfolds itself in a way such as it can do amid no other order of His creatures. There it shows itself in all its manifold fullness such as it has no scope for elsewhere. It is in the family alone that the one thing we call affection or love is divided and spread out, like a sunbeam into the rainbow's sevenfold hues, there to display itself in all the rich tints of hidden beauty. So it is in the church alone that the love of God is fully seen, not merely in all its intensity, but in all its varied riches. All kinds of love are unfolded there. There is room for such a wide variety of affection, both between the Head and the members, and between the members one with the other, that it seems as if there had been given new powers of loving as well as new objects to love.

No doubt there are other names for the saints besides this one. But none of them expresses what this is intended to do. God calls them His flock, which implies tender watchfulness on His part, and dependent helplessness on theirs. He calls them a vine, denoting their oneness, as well as the unceasing nourishment that is ever circulating through them from the parent stem. He calls them a temple, signifying their compactness of structure, symmetry of design, beauty of form, and above all, fitness for the inhabitation and worship of Jehovah. He calls them a body, to set forth, not merely their comely proportions, but their marvelous unity and conscious vitality of being, as well as the closeness of the binding tie, and their various serviceableness to each other. He calls them a city, intimating their happy community of privileges and rights and well-ordered government; the security, peace, abundance which they enjoy, the comforts of neighborhood with all its cheerful greetings and mutual offices of love. He calls them a kingdom, as expressive of their high and honorable estate, of the royalty, the glory, the dominion, of which they have been made the heirs. But various and expressive as are these well-known names, they are still imperfect. They describe as it were only the outer circles, each name a circle of its own. But the inner circle—the inner region of our spiritual being—they do not touch upon. It is that well-known word, that magic name, family, which alone can express all that God sees of what is comely and tender, loving and lovable in the church of Christ into which He is pouring His love through which He delights to see that love circulate unhindered, and out of which He expects that love to flow abroad.

There is one thing that strikes us much concerning this family. It is the way in which Christ speaks of the special interest which He takes in each member. "Those that thou gavest me I have kept, and none of them is lost" (John 17:12). How like the family feeling! Each name, each face is known; known so familiarly that the least and youngest would at once be missed. The place where each sits, the room which each occupies, the time of his going out and coming in; his looks, his habits, his tones are so thoroughly known that the moment anyone is absent, he is missed. And then no other can supply his place. His absence makes a blank which none but he can fill. An acquaintance or fellow-townsman may drop away and never be missed. His place is easily filled by another. Not so with a member of the family. Where there is a break in the circle, there is a dismal blank; and when death has carried off a brother, a sister, or a parent, who or what can ever fill his room? When one flower fades, another springs up, fresher perhaps and more fragrant—and we forget the faded one. But the withered family flower can have no successor: it dies, and there is a blank forever. Might it not be with some such feeling that Jesus looked around upon His vast household circle, and, while surveying each well-known face, gave thanks that not one was lost; as if He could not have spared so much as one of those whom the Father had given Him?

Oh, the deep interest which Jesus takes in each! Truly it is a personal and peculiar attachment for each member. Do we not lose much by forgetting this? Even in human things we are apt to overlook this. We call the feeling which the father entertains for each of his children, love; and well we call it so, but this is not all. There is a difference in the love he bears for his eldest and his youngest born, a difference in the case of each, called forth by the peculiar character of each. It is this minute and special love which is so precious. Were it not for this, we should feel as if we had only part of our father's heart, as if we had not all of that which rightfully belongs to us. But, realizing this, we feel as if we had his whole heart, and yet our having the whole did not rob our brothers and sisters of any. It is with a family as with the sun in the firmament. It is the property of all, and yet each has the whole of it. Even so with Jehovah, our heavenly Father; even so with Jesus, our elder brother. His is a special, personal, peculiar love, just as if He loved no other, but had His whole heart to spare for us. His is a minute and watchful care, bending over each, day and night, as if He had no other to care for. How sweet to think that each of us is the special object of such personal attachment, the peculiar object of such unwearied vigilance! What manner of love is this! Now we believe and are sure that we shall be fully cared for, and not one want or sorrow will be overlooked. Now we know that "all things shall work together for our good," and that the end of everything which befalls us here shall be light and glory forever! "I know the thoughts that I think towards you, saith the Lord, thoughts of peace and not of evil, to give you an expected end" (Jer. 29:11). "As one whom his mother comforteth, so will I comfort you" (Isa. 66:13). "Like as a father pitieth his children, so the Lord pitieth them that fear him" (John 15:9).

It is sweet to realize the common love flowing out of the Father's bosom to the whole happy household of His saved ones; but it is no less sweet, specially in the day of trial, to dwell upon the personal love He bears so peculiarly to each. It is blessed to identify ourselves with such a family who are all joying in the sunshine of paternal love; but it is as blessed at times to isolate oneself and realize the individual love which is our own peculiar heritage. Thus felt the Bride when she said, "Let him kiss me with the kisses of his mouth: for thy love is better than wine" (Song 1:12). "I am my beloved's, and my beloved is mine" (Song 26:3). It was when the Holy Spirit first opened our ears to listen to the tale of love which the gospel brought to us that we sought our Father's house and rested not until we had found ourselves in His embrace. It was when we first received "the gift of God," and understood the love which that gift declared, that we took our place in the family circle, tasting the plenty of our Father's table and enjoying the sweetness of our Father's smile. And even as we entered in, so are we to abide forever, "rooted and grounded in love," realizing the words of Jesus, "As the Father hath loved me, so have I loved you: continue ye in my love" (John 15:9).

2

The Family Life

They live by faith. Thus they began and thus they are to end. "We walk by faith and not by sight." Their whole life is a life of faith. Their daily actions are all of faith. This forms one of the main elements of their character. It marks them out as a peculiar people. None live as they do.

Their faith is to them "the substance of things hoped for, the evidence of things not seen." It is a sort of substitute for sight and possession. It so brings them into contact with the unseen world that they feel as if they were already conversant with, and living among, the things unseen. It makes the future, the distant, the impalpable, appear as the present, the near, the real. It removes all intervening time; it annihilates all interposing space; it transplants the soul at once into the world above. That which we know is to be hereafter is felt as if already in being. Hence, the coming of the Lord is always spoken of as at hand. Nay, more than this, the saints are represented as "having their conversation in heaven," as being already "seated with Christ in heavenly places" (Eph. 2:16), as having "come to Mount Zion, and unto the city of the living God, the heavenly Jerusalem, and to an innumerable company of angels, to the general assembly and church of the firstborn which are written in heaven, and to God the judge of all, and to the spirits of just men made perfect" (Heb. 12:22). The things amid which they are to move hereafter are so realized by faith as to appear the things amid which they are at present moving. They sit in "heavenly places" and look down upon the earth, with all its clouds and storms, as lying immeasurably far beneath their feet. And what is a "present evil world" to those who are already above all its vicissitudes and breathing a purer atmosphere?

Such is the power of faith. It throws back into the far distance the things of earth, the things that men call near and real; and it brings forward into vital contact with the soul the things which men call invisible and distant. It discloses to us the heavenly mansions, their passing splendor, their glorious purity, their blessed peace. It shows us the happy courts, the harmonious company, the adoring multitudes. It opens our ears also, so that when beholding these great sights we seem to hear the heavenly melody and to catch the very words of the new song they sing, "Thou art worthy…for thou wast slain, and hast redeemed us to God by thy blood out of every kindred, and tongue, and people, and nation; and hast made us unto our God kings and priests: and we shall reign on the earth" (Rev. 5:9).

It, moreover, points our eye forward to what is yet to come: the coming of the Lord, the judgment of the great day, the restitution of all things, the kingdom that cannot be moved, the city which hath foundations whose builder and maker is God. While thus it gives to things invisible a body and a form which before they possessed not in our eyes, on the other hand, it divests things visible of that semblance of excellence and reality with which they were formerly clothed. It strips the world of its false but bewildering glow, and enables us to penetrate the thin disguise that hides its poverty and meanness. It not only sweeps away the cloud which hung above us, obstructing our view of heavenly excellence, but it places that cloud beneath us to counteract the fallacious brightness and unreal beauty which the world has thrown over itself to mask its inward deformity.

Thus it is that faith enables us to realize our true position of pilgrims and strangers upon earth, looking for the city which hath foundations, whose builder and maker is God. It is into this that we are introduced by faith at our conversion. For what is our conversion but a turning of our back upon the world and bidding farewell to all that the heart had hitherto been entwined around? It is then that like Abraham we forsake all and go out, not knowing whither. Old ties are broken, although sometimes hard to sever. New ones are formed, although not of earth. We begin to look around us and find all things new. We feel that we are strangers— strangers in that very spot where we have been so long at home. But this is our joy. We have left our father's house, but we are hastening on to a more enduring home. We have taken leave of the world—but we have become heirs of the eternal kingdom, sons and daughters of the Lord Almighty. We have left Egypt, but Canaan is in view. We are in the wilderness, but we are free. Ours is a pathless waste, but we move forward under the shadow of the guardian cloud. Sorrowful, we yet rejoice; poor, we make many rich; having nothing, yet we possess all things. We have a rich inheritance in reversion and a long eternity in which to enjoy it without fear of loss, or change, or end.

Walking thus by faith and not by sight, what should mar our joy? Does it not come from that which is within the veil? And what storm of the desert can find entrance there? Our rejoicing is in the Lord, and He is without variableness or shadow of turning. We know that this is not our rest; neither do we wish it were so, for it is polluted; but our joy is this, that Jehovah is our God, and His promised glory is our inheritance forever. Our morning and our evening song is this "The Lord is the portion of mine inheritance and of my cup: thou maintainest my lot. The lines have fallen unto me in pleasant places; yea, I have a goodly heritage" (Ps. 16:5). Why should we, then, into whose hands the cup of gladness shall ere long be put, shrink from the vinegar and the gall? Why should we, who have dearer friends above, better bonds that cannot be dissolved, be disconsolate at the severance of an earthly tie? Our homes may be empty, our firesides may be thinned, and our hearts may bleed: but these are not enduring things; and why should we feel desolate as if all gladness had departed? Why should we, who shall wear a crown and inherit all things, sigh or fret because of a few years' poverty and shame? Earth's dream will soon be done; and then comes the day of "songs and everlasting joy"—the long reality of bliss! Jesus will soon be here; and "when he who is our life shall appear, then shall we also appear with him in glory." Shall trial shake us? Nay, in all this we are more than conquerors through Him that loved us. Shall sorrow move us? Faith tells us of a land where sorrow is unknown. Shall the death of saints move us? Faith tells us not to sorrow as those who have no hope, for if we believe that Jesus died and rose again, them also that sleep in Jesus will God bring with Him. Shall the pains and weariness of this frail body move us? Faith tells us of a time at hand when this corruptible shall put on incorruption, and death shall be swallowed up in victory. Shall privation move us? Faith tells us of a day when the poverty of our exile shall be forgotten in the abundance of our peaceful, plenteous home, where we shall hunger no more, neither thirst any more.

Shall the disquieting bustle of this restless life annoy us? Faith tells us of the rest that remaineth for the people of God—the sea of glass like unto crystal on which the ransomed saints shall stand—no tempest, no tumult, no shipwreck there. Shall the lack of this world's honors move us? Faith tells us of the exceeding and eternal weight of glory in reserve. Have we no place to lay our head? Faith tells us that we have a home, though not in Caesar's house, a dwelling, though not in any city of earth. Are we fearful as we look around upon the disorder and wretchedness of this misgoverned earth? Faith tells us that the coming of the Lord draweth nigh. Do thoughts of death alarm us? Faith tells us that "to die is gain," and whispers to us, "What, are you afraid of becoming immortal, afraid of passing from this state of death, which men call life, to that which alone truly deserves the name!"

Such is the family life—a life of faith. We live upon things unseen. Our life is hid with Christ in God, that when He who is our life shall appear, we may appear with Him in glory. This mode of life is not that of the world at all but the very opposite. Nevertheless, it has been that of the saints from the beginning. This is the way in which they have walked, going up through the wilderness leaning on their Beloved. And such is to be the walk of the saints till the Lord comes. Oh, how much is there in these thoughts concerning it, not only to reconcile us to it, but to make us rejoice in it, and to say, I reckon that the sufferings of this present life are not worthy to be compared with the glory which shall be revealed in us! For all things are ours, whether life or death, things present or things to come, all are ours; for we are Christ's, and Christ is God's. Yea, we are heirs of God, and joint-heirs with Jesus Christ. "This is the heritage of the servants of the Lord, and their righteousness is of me, saith the Lord" (Isa. 54:17).

We know not a better type or specimen of the family life than Abraham or Israel in their desert wanderings. Look at Abraham. He quits all at the command of the God of glory. This begins his life of faith. Then he journeys onward not knowing whither. Then he sojourns as a stranger in the land which God had given him. Then he offers up Isaac. Then he buys for himself a tomb where he may lay his dust till the day of resurrection. All is faith. He lives and acts as a stranger. He has no home. He has his altar and his tent, but that is all—the one he builds wherever he goes, in the peaceful consciousness of sin forgiven and acceptance found; the other he pitches from day to day in token of his being a pilgrim and a stranger upon earth. And what more does any member of the family need below, but his altar and his tent—a Savior for a sinful soul, and a shelter for a frail body until journeying days are done? Or look at Israel. They quit Egypt. There the life of faith begins. Then they cross the Red Sea. Then they take up their abode in the desert. They have no city to dwell in now. They have no fleshpots now—nothing but the daily manna for food. They have no river of Egypt now—nothing but a rock to yield them water. All is waste around. All is to be of faith, not of sight. They are alone with God, and the whole world is afar off. They rear their altar, they pitch their tents, as did Abraham, with this only difference: above their heads there floats a wondrous cloud, which, like a heavenly canopy, stretches itself out over their dwellings when they rest, or like an angel-guide, it takes wing before them when God summons them to strike their tents that it may lead them in the way. Nay, and as if to mark more vividly the pilgrim condition of the family, God Himself, when coming down into the midst of them, chooses a tent to dwell in. It is called "the tabernacle of the Lord," or more literally "Jehovah's tent." Jehovah pitches His tent side by side with Israel's tents, as if He were a stranger too, a wanderer like themselves!

This is our life. We are to be strangers with God as all our fathers were. It is the life of the desert, not of the city. But what of that? All is well. Jehovah is our God, and we shall soon be in His "many mansions." Meanwhile, we have the tent, the altar, and the cloud. We need no more below. The rest is secured for us in heaven, "ready to be revealed in the last time."

3

The Family Badge

The family of which we speak is gathered out of every nation and kindred, and people, and tongue. It is "a great multitude that no man can number."

Yet it is but one family. There is a family likeness among all its many members; and a family name by which they are known. They have many things in common; nay, there are few things which are not common to all. They are all of earth. It is their native clime. They are all sprinkled with the same blood and begotten again by the same Spirit. They all sing one song, use one language, rejoice in one hope, and are heirs of one inheritance. This oneness of feature and feeling and habit, throughout so many ages and amid so many diverse nations, marks them out as a peculiar people and reveals their relationship to Him who is "the same yesterday, and today and forever."

But they have one mark more peculiar than any of these. It is truly a family badge: they are all cross-bearers. This is the unfailing token by which each member may be recognized. They all bear a cross. Nor do they hide it as if ashamed of it. They make it their boast. "God forbid that we should glory, save in the cross of our Lord Jesus Christ, by whom the world is crucified to us, and we unto the world." Sometimes it is lighter, and sometimes it is heavier; sometimes it has more of shame and suffering, and sometimes less, but still it is upon them. They carry it with them wherever they go. And it is always a cross: not merely so in name, but in reality, a token of reproach and sorrow. Sometimes they are represented as carrying it, and sometimes as being nailed to it, but it is still the cross.

They took it up when first they believed in Jesus and owned Him as their all. Then it was that they forsook the world's tents and went without the gate, bearing the reproach of the crucified One. He whom they follow both bore the cross and was nailed to it, and why should they shrink from the like endurance? Shall they be ashamed of Him? Shall they not rather count it honorable to follow where He has led the way, and to bear for Him some faint resemblance of what He bore for them? Shall anything in the world be esteemed more precious, more honorable than the cross of their beloved Lord? The world derides and despises it, but it is the cross of Jesus; and that is all to them. A saint of other days, a cross-bearer of the olden time, has said, "O blessed cross of Christ, there is no wood like thine!"

Besides, this was the Master's will. He has laid on each the command to bear the cross. "If any man will come after me, let him deny himself, and take up his cross daily, and follow me" (Luke 9:23). "He that taketh not his cross, and followeth after me, is not worthy of me" (Matt. 10:38). The cross, then, is the badge of discipleship, and no follower of the Lord can be without it. The two things are inseparable. God has joined them, and man cannot sunder them. No cross, no saint. No cross, no Son. We must carry His cross all our life; we must be baptized with His baptism; we must endure His reproach; we must glory in being clothed with His shame. The flesh must be crucified with its affections and lusts: our members must be mortified; our old man must take the place of shame; we in whom the flesh still remaineth, though its dominion is broken, must be willing to appear as outcasts and malefactors before the world, as Jesus did when He bore our sins upon the hill of shame. Jesus, then, with His own hand lays the cross on each one who comes to Him, saying, "Take this and follow me. Take it and be reproached for Me. Take it and endure tribulation for Me. Take it, and count all things but loss for the excellency of the knowledge of Jesus Christ thy Lord. Take it and be willing to go even to prison or to death for Me, not counting your life dear unto you, that you may follow Me to the end and receive the unfading crown." Learn to endure the cross and to despise the shame.

But further, we have the Master's example as well as the Master's will concerning this. I do not mean merely that He hung upon the cross. I do not refer simply to the fact of His crucifixion. I mean much more than that. That was but the closing scene of a whole life of crucifixion. He was a cross-bearer from the hour that He was laid in the manger. All His days He bore the cross. His life was but a pilgrimage to Calvary with the cross upon His shoulders. Tradition tells us that, as He left the Judgment Hall, He was led along the "dolorous way" to Golgotha. But in truth, His whole course on earth was the mournful way. It was all reproach and sorrow from His cradle to His grave. His was a sorrowing life; His death was but the summing up of His many sorrows, the gathering of them all together and pressing them into His cup at once, till the vessel burst, because it could hold no more. And then, for Him, the cross and the shame and the sorrow were at an end forever. But for us the cross remaineth still.

Throughout life He was the "man of sorrows." He was "acquainted with grief." And herein we see something more of the family badge as it was displayed in the Elder Brother: acquaintanceship with grief! This is the description given us of it. It is not one visit that makes us acquainted with a fellow-man. Companionship is the result of continued intercourse. So one sorrow does not make us acquainted with grief, however deep and sharp its pangs may be. It may be the beginning of our acquaintanceship, but that is all. There must be daily, hourly intercourse. Thus it was with Jesus. Thirty-three years daily converse with grief made Him acquainted with it. And so it is with us. The saints are men of sorrows still; and their acquaintanceship with grief must be obtained by daily fellowship. The disciple is not above his Master, nor the servant above his Lord. We need not think of another process than that which He underwent. He was made perfect through sufferings, and so must we. The Captain of our salvation is, in this respect, the model and pattern of His saved ones. We are always to bear "about in the body the dying of the Lord Jesus, that the life also of Jesus might be made manifest in our body" (2 Cor. 4:10).

It is the Lamb that we follow: the Lamb "as it had been slain." This surely speaks most plainly of the family badge. We are followers of the Man with the pierced hands and feet, the Man who is covered all over with the marks of the buffet and the scourge and the spitting, the Man with the crown of thorns. Yea, He is our Elder Brother. He is bone of our bone and flesh of our flesh. And if we see so distinctly the family badge on Him, shall we shrink from taking it up and binding it in triumph as a jewel on our forehead—as a crown upon our head? Surely the purple robe of mockery may beseem us better than it suited Him.

There is one mark by which, from the beginning, he has been distinguished as the woman's seed predicted in Eden. It is the bruised heel. This is, in truth, only another way of expressing His character as the suffering, the crucified Son of Man. This was the mark which God gave by which He was to be known. Yet it was just at this stumbling stone that Israel stumbled. They had no eyes for the dying Savior. The humbled Jesus found no favor with them. The bruised heel they could not away with. The very mark which God set upon Him as Messiah was that on account of which Israel rejected Him. Yet it is the bruised heel in which we rejoice.

It is the Man with the bruised heel who has won our hearts. It is He whom we follow; and His bruised heel we engrave upon our banner as our most honorable badge.

The similar bruising we look for as our portion here. Nor are we ashamed of it. All the saints before us have experienced it; are we better than they? Shall the soldiers of the last days be ashamed to wear the uniform which the army of the saints has gloried in for six thousand years?

It is very remarkable that the apostle fixes upon affliction as the mark of true sonship. Truly, he makes it the family badge. Nay, he makes it the test of our legitimacy. "What son is he whom the father chasteneth not? But if ye be without chastisement, whereof all are partakers, then are ye bastards, and not sons" (Heb. 12:7, 8). Strong language this! Had any but an inspired apostle used it, there would have been outcry against it as absurd and extravagant. Let us, however, take it as it is, for we know that it speaks the mind of God. Chastisement is, then, really one of the chief marks of our lawful and honorable birth. Were this characteristic not to be found on us, we should be lacking in one of the proofs of our sonship. Our legitimacy might be called in question. It might be said that He was not recognizing us as His true-born sons, and that either He had never received us as such, or had rejected us. There must be the family badge to establish our claim of birth and to be a pledge of paternal recognition on the part of God our Father.

It is a solemn thought. Flesh and blood shrink from it. We look around to see if there be no way of escaping, and ask if it must be so. Yes, it must be, as we shall shortly see, and the attempt to shun it is vain. Yet it is also a blessed thought. It cheers us under trial to remember that this is the Father's seal set upon His true-born sons. Oh, how it lightens the load to think that it is really the pledge of our divine adoption!

We need not then count upon bright days below, nor think to pass lightly over the pleasant earth as if our life were but the "shadow of a dream." Joy within we may expect—"joy unspeakable and full of glory"—for that is the family portion. But joy from without, the joy of earth's sunshine, the joy of the world's ease and abundance, the joy of unsevered bonds and unweeping eyes is not our lot in this vale of tears. Still, in the midst of the ever-wakeful storms through which we are passing to the kingdom, there is peace—deep peace—too deep for any storm of earth to reach. In the world we have tribulation, but in Jesus we have peace. "Peace I leave with you, my peace I give unto you, not as the world giveth give I unto you." And it is this which gives the peculiar aspect to the saints, the aspect of mingled joy and grief. The eye is dim with tears, yet, behold, it glistens with joy! There is the brow of shaded thought, yet peace is playing round it. Clouds overshadow them, but on every cloud we see calm sunshine resting.

Their "peace is like a river." It is not stagnant as the lake, nor tumultuous as the sea, but ever in calm motion, ever flowing on in its deep channel like a river. The course may sometimes be through rocks, sometimes through level plains, sometimes through tangled brakes, sometimes along the cornfield or "the hill of vines," yet still it moves unhindered on. It may be night or day, it may be winter or summer, it may be storm or calm, but it is there—flowing on till the embrace of ocean receives it. Such is our peace! Let us hold it fast.

Nor need we hide our peace any more than we should hide our cross. Let the world see both and learn how well they agree together. For it is the cross that makes this peace feel so sweet and suitable. Amid the tears of grief peace keeps her silent place like the rainbow upon the spray of the cataract; nor can it be driven thence so long as Jehovah's sunshine rests upon the soul. "The work of righteousness shall be peace, and the effect of righteousness, quietness and assurance forever."

4

The Family Discipline

"Train up a child in the way he should go" is the injunction God lays on us. But it is, moreover, the principle on which He Himself is acting with His church. He is training up His children here. This is the true character of His dealings with them. The education of His saints is the object He has in view. It is training for the kingdom; it is education for eternity.

How momentous, then, is the training! It is God who is carrying it on by the Holy Ghost. It is the church, which is the Body of Christ, that is the subject of it. And it is to prepare her for an everlasting kingdom. In bringing many sons unto glory, it was needful that even the Captain of their salvation should be made perfect through suffering. Surely, then, God lays vast stress upon this discipline. In His estimation it is no unimportant nor unmeaning exercise. Knowing this, the apostle exhorts us on this very point, "My son, despise not thou the chastening of the Lord." It is too solemn to be despised, too momentous to be overlooked. The education of God's family is concerned with it. The preparation of an heir of glory depends on it.

This discipline begins at our conversion. The moment we are taken into the family it commences. "He scourgeth every son whom he receiveth." It is not always visible; neither are we at all times conscious of its operation. Nevertheless, from the very day that "we are begotten again to a lively hope" it begins. It ends only with life, or in the case of the last generation of the church, with their being "caught up to meet the Lord in the air." It is a whole lifetime's process. It is a daily, an hourly discipline which admits of no cessation. The rod may not always be applied, but still the discipline goes on.

1. *It is the discipline of love.* Every step of it is kindness. There is no wrath or vengeance in any part of the process. The discipline of the school may be harsh and stern, but that of the family is love. We are sure of this; and the consolation which it affords is unutterable. Love will not wrong us. There will be no needless suffering. Were this but kept in mind there would be fewer hard thoughts of God among men, even when His strokes are most severe. I know not a better illustration of what the feelings of a saint should be, in the hour of bitterness, than the case of Richard Cameron's father. The aged saint was in prison "for the Word of God and the testimony of Jesus Christ." The bleeding head of his martyred son was brought to him by his unfeeling persecutors, and he was asked derisively if he knew it. "I know it, I know it," said the father, as he kissed the mangled forehead of his fair-haired son, "it is my son's; my own dear son's! It is the Lord! Good is the will of the Lord, who cannot wrong me or mine, but who hath made goodness and mercy to follow us all our days."

2. *It is the discipline of wisdom.* He who administers it is the "God only wise." What deep wisdom then must there be in all His dealings! He knows exactly what we need and how to supply it. He knows what evils are to be found in us, and how these may be best removed. His training is no random work. It is carried on with exquisite skill. The time and the way and the instrument are all according to the perfect wisdom of God. The fittest time is chosen, just the very moment when discipline is called for, and when it would be most profitable.

The surest, most direct, and at the same time gentlest method is devised. The instrument which will be surest yet safest, most effectual yet least painful, is brought into operation. For all is wisdom in the discipline of God.

3. *It is the discipline of faithfulness.* "In faithfulness thou hast afflicted me," said David. All is the doing of a faithful God— a God who is faithful to us as well as faithful to Himself. "Faithful are the wounds of a friend," says Solomon; and the believer finds in trouble the faithfulness of the truest of friends. He is so faithful that He will not pass by a single fault that He sees in us, but will forthwith make it known that it may be removed. He gave this command to Israel, "Thou shalt in any wise rebuke thy neighbor, and not suffer sin upon him," (Lev. 19:17) and He Himself acts upon the command He gave. He is too faithful a Father to suffer sin upon His children unreproved. He is true to us, whether in sending the evil or the good; shall we not say, truer and more faithful when He inflicts the evil than when He bestows the good? It almost at times seems to break the heart of a loving friend to be obliged to say or do anything severe toward the friend he loves. Yet for love's sake he will do it. In faithfulness he will not shrink from it. And in doing so, is he not true to his friend? So with a chastening God. He is faithful when He blesses—more faithful when He chastens. This surely is consolation. It may well allay all murmuring and establish our hearts in peace.

4. *It is the discipline of power.* He who is carrying it on is not one who can be baffled and forced to give up His design. He is able to carry it out in the unlikeliest circumstances and against the most resolute resistance. Everything must give way before Him. This thought is, I confess, to me one of the most comforting connected with the discipline. If it could fail, if God could be frustrated in His designs after we have suffered so much, it would be awful! To be scourged and suffer pain

by one who is not able to make good to us the profit of this would add inconceivable bitterness to the trial. And then our hearts are so hard, our wills so stubborn, that nothing save an Almighty pressure applied to them can work the desired change. Oh, when the soul is at strife within itself, battling in desperate conflict with its stormy lusts, when the flesh rises up in its strength and refuses to yield, when the whole heart appears like iron or is adamant, it is most blessed to think upon God's chastisements as the discipline of power! It is this that assures us that all shall yet be well. And it is in the strength of this assurance that we gird ourselves for the battle, knowing that we must be more than conquerors through Him that loved us.

There might be love in the dealing—love to the uttermost—and yet all be in vain. For love is oftentimes helpless, unable to do aught for the beloved object. There might be wisdom, too, and yet it might prove wholly ineffectual. There might also be untiring faithfulness, yet no results. It might be altogether impotent even in its fondest vigilance. It might be baffled in its most earnest attempts to bless. But when it is infinite power that is at work, we are sure of every obstacle being surmounted, and everything that is blessed coming most surely to pass. My sickbed may be most lovingly tended, most skillfully provided for, most faithfully watched, and I may be most sweetly soothed by this fond and unwearied care; yet, if there be no power to heal, no resistless energy such as sweeps all hindrances before it, then I may still lie hopeless there; but, if the power to heal be present, the power that makes all diseases flee its touch, the power that, if need be, can raise the dead, then I know of a truth that all is well.

Oh, it is blessed and comforting to remember that it is the discipline of power that is at work upon us! God's treatment must succeed. It cannot miscarry or be frustrated even in its most arduous efforts, even in reference to its minutest objects. It is the mighty power of God that is at work within us and upon us, and this is our consolation. It is the grasp of an infinite hand that is upon us, and nothing can resist its pressure. All is love, all is wisdom, and all is faithfulness, yet all is also power. The very possibility of failure is thus taken away. Were it not for this power there could be no certainty of blessing, and were it not for this certainty, how poor and partial would our comfort be! He, yes, He who chastises us is "able to do exceeding abundantly above all that we ask or think, according to the power that worketh in us" (Eph. 3:20).

Hence to a soul, conscious of utter helplessness and weary of the struggle within between the spirit and the flesh, there is "strong consolation" in remembering the power of Him whose hand is now grasping him so firmly on every side. His sorely tossed spirit finds peace in calling to mind "the years of the right hand of the Most High"—all the "works of the Lord and his wonders of old." The "strength of Israel" is the name he delights in, as the name of his Chastener. He thus bethinks himself, "The God who made these heavens and stretched them out in their vastness and majesty, who moves these stars in their courses and arrests them at a word, is the God who is chastening me. He who raises and stills the mighty deep and all the multitude of its waves, the God of the tempest and of the earthquake, 'the framer of light and dark, the wielder of the lightning and the builder of the everlasting hills,' is the God who is now laying His rod so heavily upon me." Thus each new proof or aspect of Jehovah's power becomes a new source of consolation in the day of chastisement and sorrow.

Such, then, is the nature of the family discipline when viewed in reference to God. Love, wisdom, faithfulness, and power unite to devise and carry it out. It must, then, be perfect discipline, the completest and most successful that can be thought of or desired. It is well to look at it in this light, for it is thus that we become entirely satisfied with all that comes to pass and feel that "it is well." But let us consider it in another aspect. We have seen what it is when flowing out of God; let us see what it is when operating upon man.

As we observed before, God's object in chastisement is the education of His children, the training up of the saints. It is their imperfect spiritual condition that makes this so necessary. And now we proceed to inquire in what way it works, and toward what regions of the soul it is specially directed. For while, doubtless, it embraces the whole soul in all its parts and powers, it may be well to consider it as more especially set to work upon its mind, its will, its heart, and its conscience.

1. *It is the training of the mind.* We are naturally most unteachable as well as most ignorant, neither knowing anything nor willing to know. The ease of prosperous days augments the evil. God at length interposes and compels us to learn. "The rod and reproof give wisdom" (Prov. 29:15). He sends trial and that makes us willing to learn. Our unteachableness gives way. We become aware of our ignorance. We seek teaching from on high. God begins His work of instruction. Light pours in on every side. We grow amazingly in knowledge. We learn the meaning of words now which we had hitherto used but as familiar sounds. Scripture shines out before us in new effulgence; it flashes into us; every verse seems to contain a sunbeam; dark places become light; every promise stands out in illuminated splendor; things hard to be understood become in a moment plain.

How fast we learn in a day of sorrow! It is as if affliction awoke our powers and lent them new quickness of perception. We advance more in the knowledge of Scripture in a single day than in years before. We learn "songs in the night," though such music was unknown before. A deeper experience has taken us down into the depths of Scripture and shown us its hidden wonders. Luther used to say, "Were it not for tribulation I should not understand Scripture." And every sorrowing saint responds to this, as having felt its truth—felt it as did David, when he said, "Blessed is the man whom thou chastenest...and teachest him out of thy law" (Ps. 94:12). "It is good for me that I have been afflicted; that I might learn thy statutes" (Ps. 119:71). What teaching, what training of the mind goes on upon a sickbed, or under the pressure of grief! And, oh, what great and wondrous things will even some little trial whisper in the ear of a soul that is "learning of the Father"!

In some cases this profit is almost unfelt, at least during the continuance of the process. We think that we are learning nothing. Sorrow overwhelms us. Disaster stuns us. We become confused, nervous, agitated, or perhaps insensible. We seem to derive no profit. Yet ere long we begin to feel the blessed results. Maturity of judgment, patience in listening to the voice of God, a keener appetite for His Word, a quicker discernment of its meaning—these are soon realized as the gracious results of chastisement. The mind has undergone a most thorough discipline, and has, moreover, made wondrous progress in the knowledge of divine truth through the teaching of the Holy Ghost.

2. *It is the training of the will.* The will is the seat of rebelliousness. Here the warfare is carried on. "The flesh lusteth against the spirit, and the spirit against the flesh." At conversion the will is bent in the right direction, but it is still crooked and rigid. Rebelliousness is still there. Prosperous days may sometimes conceal it so that we are almost unconscious of its strength. But it still exists. Furnace heat is needed for softening and strengthening it. No milder remedy will do. "It requires," says a suffering saint, "all the energy of God to bend my will to His." Yet it must be done. The will is the soul's citadel. Hence, it is the will that God seems so specially to aim at in chastisement. Fire after fire does He kindle in order to soften it; and blow after blow does He fetch down on it to straighten it. Nor does He rest till He has made it thoroughly flexible and hammered out of it the many relics

of self which it contains. He will not stay His hand till He has thoroughly marred our self-formed plans and shown us the folly of our self-chosen ways.

This is specially the case in long-continued trials; either when these come stroke after stroke in sad succession, or when one fearful stroke at the outset has left behind it consequences which years perhaps will not fully unfold. The bending and straightening of the will is often a long process, during which the soul has to pass through waters deep and many, through fires hot and ever kindling up anew. Protracted trials seem specially aimed at the will. Its perversity and stiffness can only be wrought out of it by a long succession of trials. It is only by degrees that it becomes truly pliable and is brought into harmony with the will of God. We can at a stroke lop off the unseemly branch; but to give a proper bent to the tree itself, we require time and assiduous appliances for months or years. Yet the will must give way. However proud, however forward, it must bend. God will not leave it till He has made it one with His own.[1]

3. *It is the training of the heart.* Man's heart beats false to God. It is true to many things but false to Him. When first the Holy Spirit touches it, and shows it "the exceeding riches of the grace of God," then it becomes in some measure true. Yet it is only in part. Much false-heartedness still remains. It clings too fondly to the creature. It cleaves to the dust. It is not wholly God's. But this cannot be. God must have the heart; nay, and He must have it beating truly toward Him. He is jealous of our love, and grieves over its feebleness or its falling away. It is love that He wants, and with nothing but truehearted love will He be satisfied. For this it is that He chastises. These false throbbings of the heart; these goings out after other objects than Himself He cannot suffer but must correct or else forego His claim. Hence, He smites and

---

1. "Character is a perfectly educated will," says a German writer.

spares not till He has made us sensible of our guilt in this respect. He strips off the leaves whose beauty attracted us; He cuts down the flowers whose fragrance fascinated us; He tears off one string after another from the lyre whose music charmed us. Then when He has showed us each object of earth in its nakedness or deformity, then He presents Himself to us in the brightness of His own surpassing glory. And thus He wins the heart. Thus He makes it true to Him. Thus He makes us ashamed of our false-heartedness to Himself and to the Son of His love.

Yet this is no easy process. This training is hard and sore. The heart bleeds under it. Yet it must go on. No part of it can be spared. Nor will it cease till the heart is won! If the Chastener should stay His hand before this is effected, where would be His love? What poor, what foolish affection! He knew this when He said, "Let them alone"; and it was the last thing that His love consented to do, after all else had failed. One of the sharpest, sorest words He ever spoke to Israel was, "Why should ye be stricken any more?" Let us remember this, and not faint, even though the heart has been long bleeding. Let us remember it, and seek to make the sorrow shorter by gladly joining with Him in His plan for getting possession of our whole heart. We need not grudge it. He has "good measure" to give us in return. His love will taste the sweeter, and it will abide and satisfy us forever. It is well for us to be thus trained to love Him here, with whom, in love and fellowship unbroken, we are to spend the everlasting day.

4. *It is the training of the conscience.* A seared conscience is the sinner's heritage. It is upon this that the Holy Spirit first lays His hand when He awakens the soul from its sleep of death. He touches the conscience, and then the struggles of conviction come. He then pacifies it by the sprinkling of the blood, showing it Jesus and His cross. Then giving it to taste forgiveness, it rests from all its tumults and fears. Thoughts of peace are ever breathed into it from the sight of the

bleeding sacrifice. It trembles no more, for it sees that that which made it tremble is the very thing concerning which the blood of Christ speaks peace. "Their sins and their iniquities will I remember no more." Thus it is softened. Its first terrors upon awakening could not be called a softening. But now conscious forgiveness and realized peace with God have been to it like the mild breath of spring to the ice of winter. It has become soft and tender, yet only so in part.

God's desire, however, is to make it altogether tender. He wishes it to be sensitive in regard to the very touch of sin, and earnest in its pantings after perfect holiness. To effect this, He afflicts; and affliction goes directly home to the conscience. The death of the widow's son at Sarepta immediately awakened her conscience, and she cried to the prophet, "O man of God, art thou come to call my sin to remembrance?" (1 Kings 17:18). So God by chastisement lays His finger upon the conscience, and forthwith it springs up into new life. We are made to feel as if God had now come down to us, as if He were now looking into our hearts and commencing a narrow search. Moreover, we see in this affliction God's estimate of sin. Not, indeed, the full estimate. No, that we only learn from the sufferings of Jesus. But still we gather from this new specimen of sin's bitter fruits somewhat of His mind regarding sin. This teaches the conscience by making the knowledge of sin a thing of experience—an experience that is deepening with every new trial. "If they be bound in fetters, and be holden in cords of affliction; then he showeth them their work, and their transgressions that they have exceeded. He openeth also their ear to discipline, and commandeth that they return from iniquity" (Job 36:8–10).

In these last days how little is there of tenderness of conscience! The world seems to know nothing of it save the name. It is a world without a conscience! And how much do we find the church of Christ a partaker in the world's sins! "Evil communications corrupt good manners." It is sad to observe in many saints, amid much zeal and energy and love, the lack of a tender conscience. For this God is smiting us, and will smite us yet more heavily until He has made it thoroughly tender and sensitive all over, "hating even the garments spotted by the flesh." This training of the conscience is a thing of far greater moment than many deem it. God will not rest till He has wrought it. And if the saints still continue to overlook it, if they will not set themselves in good earnest to ask for it, and to strive against everything that would tend to produce searedness and insensibility, they may yet expect some of the sharpest strokes that the hand of God has ever yet administered.

Such, then, is the family discipline. We have seen it as it comes forth from God, and we have seen it as it operates upon man. And is it not all well? What is there about it that should disquiet us, or call forth one murmur either of the lip or heart? That which opens up to us so much more of God and lets us more fully into the secrets of His heart must be blessed, however hard to bear. That which discovers to us the evils within ourselves, which makes us teachable and wise, which gives to the stiff will, flexibility and obedience, which teaches the cold heart to love and expands each straitened affection, which melts the callous conscience into tender sensitiveness, which trains up the whole soul for the glorious kingdom—that must be precious indeed.

Besides, it is the Father's will; and is not this enough for the trustful child? Is not chastisement just one of the methods by which He intimates to us what He would have us to be? Is not His way of leading us to the kingdom the safest, surest, shortest way? It is still the paternal hand that is guiding us. What though in seeking to lift us up to a higher level, it has to lay hold of us with a firmer, or it may be a rougher grasp? It is still the paternal voice "that speaketh unto us as unto children"—dear children—only in a louder, sharper tone to constrain the obedience of His too reluctant sons.

One remark more would I add to these concerning this family discipline. It is not designed even for a moment to separate them and their God, or to overshadow their souls with one suspicion of their Father's heart. That it has done so at times, I know; but that it ought never to do so I am most firmly persuaded. Is it not one of the tests of sonship, and shall that, without which we are not accounted sons, make us doubt our sonship, or suspect the love of our God? That love claims at all times, whether in sorrow or in joy, our simple, full-hearted, peaceful confidence. It is at all times the same, and chastisement is but a more earnest expression of its infinite sincerity and depth. Let us do justice to it, and to Him out of whom it flows. Let us not give it the unworthy treatment which it too often receives at our thankless hands. Let us beware of "falling from grace" at the very time when God is coming down to us to spread out before us more largely than before all the treasures of His grace. "We have known and believed the love that God hath to us," is to be our song. It ought always to be the family song! And shall it cease or sink low at the very time when it ought to be loudest and strongest? Should not trial just draw from us the apostle's triumphant boast: "Who shall separate us from the love of Christ? shall tribulation, or distress, or persecution, or famine, or nakedness, or peril, or sword?" "Nay, in all these things we are more than conquerors through him that loved us; for I am persuaded that neither death, nor life, nor angels, nor principalities, nor powers, nor things present, nor things to come, nor height, nor depth, nor any other creature, shall be able to separate us from the love of God, which is in Christ Jesus our Lord" (Rom. 8:35–39). For is it not just when we are brought under chastening that we enter upon the realities of consolation, the certainties of love, and the joys of heavenly fellowship in ways unknown and unimagined before?

5

The Family Rods

We hear of the "rod of the wicked," and we are told that it "shall not rest upon the lot of the righteous" (Ps. 125:3). This may mean that wicked men are God's rod for chastening His people, and that, though permitted to light upon them, it shall not rest or abide upon them, but shall be destroyed, as was the Assyrian, who was used by God as the "rod of his anger" for afflicting Israel. In this sense it gives us the blessed assurance that the triumph of the wicked over the saints is short, that their devices and oppressions shall last but for a moment, and that the church's sufferings at their hands shall soon be over. Wicked men may be the sword of God (Ps. 17:13), as was Pilate, when he lifted the sword against the man that was Jehovah's friend, or as Herod was when he beheaded John in prison; but that sword shall soon be broken. A wound now and then it may inflict, but that is all. It neither moves nor smites save when God allows. Nor does it come, save with a blessing on its edge. "They mean it not so," yet God means it, and that is enough for us. He makes the wrath of man to praise Him. "There shall no evil happen to the just; when he shall hear of evil tidings he shall not be afraid."

But the "rod of the wicked" may mean that rod with which He smites the wicked in His fierce anger. In this sense there is no rod for the righteous. Such a rod never either lights upon them nor rests upon them. Their rod is not the rod of the wicked. It is the family rod. They have done with wrath. Over them no curse can ever rest. "There is...no condemnation to them that are in Christ Jesus." The rod may seem to speak of frowns and anger, but it is only a seeming; there is not a glance of vengeance in the Chastener's eye. It is a correcting rod, but not a destroying one. Its object is not to punish but to chasten; not to injure but to bless. "God distributeth sorrows in his anger," (Job 21:17) but these are not for His saints.

God has, however, not one rod for His children, but many. For each child He has a peculiar rod, and at different times He uses different rods. It will be profitable for us to consider what those are, and how they are applied.

1. *Bodily sickness.* The body operates very powerfully upon the soul both for good and for evil. In what way or to what extent we cannot tell. Nor do I wish to discuss this question at all. But, knowing how the soul is acted on by the body, I cannot help think that one of God's designs in sickness is to operate upon the soul through the body. We are not conscious of this; we cannot analyze the process; the effects are hidden from view. Yet it does seem as if sickness of body were made to contribute directly to the health of the soul in some way or other known only to God. Hence, the apostle speaks of delivering "such an one unto Satan for the destruction of the flesh, that the spirit may be saved in the day of the Lord Jesus" (1 Cor. 5:5). On this point, however, I do not dwell; only it would be well for us to consider whether God is not by this intimating to us the exceeding danger of pampering the flesh: for the weakening of the flesh does help forward the strengthening of the spirit; and the mortifying of our members which are upon the earth—the crucifying the flesh with its affections and lusts—does tend to quicken and

invigorate the soul. Apart from this, however, there are other things to be kept in view.

Sickness prostrates us. It cuts into the very center of our carnal nature; it exposes in all their deformity "the lust of the flesh, the lust of the eye, and the pride of life." What vanity is seen in these upon a sickbed! These are our three idols; and these, sickness dashes down into the dust.

Sickness takes us aside and sets us alone with God. We are taken into His private chamber, and there He converses with us face to face. The world is far off, our relish for it is gone, and we are alone with God. Many are the words of grace and truth which He then speaks to us. All our former props are struck away, and we must now lean on God alone. The things of earth are felt to be vanity; man's help useless. Man's praise and man's sympathy desert us; we are cast wholly upon God that we may learn that His praise and His sympathy are enough. "If it were not for pain," says one, "I should spend less time with God. If I had not been kept awake with pain, I should have lost one of the sweetest experiences I ever had in my life. The disorder of my body is the very help I want from God; and if it does its work before it lays me in the dust, it will raise me up to Heaven." It was thus that Job was "chastened upon his bed with pain, and the multitude of his bones with strong pain," that after being tried he might "come forth as gold" (Job 23:10). Sickness teaches that activity of service is not the only way in which God is glorified. "They also serve who only stand and wait." Active duty is that which man judges most acceptable; but God shows us that in bearing and suffering He is also glorified. Perhaps we were pursuing a path of our own and required to be arrested. Perhaps we were too much harassed by a bustling world and needed retirement, yet could find no way of obtaining it till God laid us down, and drew us aside into a desert place, because of the multitude pressing upon us.

No one of the family rods is more in use than this,

sometimes falling lightly on us, at other times more heavily. Let us kiss the rod. Let us open our mouth wide to the blessing, seeking so to profit by each bodily ailment, slight or severe, that it may bring forth in us the peaceable fruits of righteousness. "I know," says one, "of no greater blessing than health, except pain and sickness."

2. *Bereavement.* This is the bitterest of all earthly sorrows. It is the sharpest arrow in the quiver of God. To love tenderly and deeply and then to part; to meet together for the last time on earth; to bid farewell for time; to have all past remembrances of home and kindred broken up—this is the reality of sorrow. To look upon that face that shall smile on us no more; to close those eyes that shall see us no more; to press those lips that shall speak to us no more; to stand by the cold side of father, mother, brother, sister, friend, yet hear no sound and receive no greeting; to carry to the tomb the beloved of our hearts, and then to return to a desolate home with a blank in one region of our souls, which shall never again be filled till Jesus come with all His saints; this is the bitterness of grief; this is the wormwood and the gall!

It is this rod which ever and anon God is laying upon us. Nor is there any that we need more than this. By it He is making room for Himself in hearts that had been filled with other objects and engrossed with other loves. He is jealous of our affection, for He claims it all as His own; and every idol He will utterly abolish. For our sakes as well as for His own He can suffer no rival in the heart. Perhaps the joys of an earthly home are stealing away our hearts from the many mansions above. God breaks in upon us in mercy and turns that home into a wilderness. Our sin finds us out; we mourn over it and seek anew to realize our heavenly citizenship and set out anew upon our pilgrim way, alone and yet not alone, for the Father is with us. Perhaps we are sitting "at ease in Zion," comfortable and contented, amid the afflictions of a suffering church and the miseries of a world that owns no Savior and fears no God. Jehovah speaks and we awake. He takes to Himself some happy saint, or smites to the dust some wretched sinner. We are troubled at the stroke. We mourn our lethargy. While we slept, a fellow-saint has gone up to be with Christ, and a fellow-sinner has gone down to be with the devil and his angels. The death of the one stirs us up; the death of the other solemnizes and overawes us. Thus as saint after saint ascends to God, we begin to feel that heaven is far more truly the family home than earth. We have far more brethren above than we have below. And each bereavement reminds us of this. It reminds us, too, that the coming of the Lord draweth nigh, and makes us look out more wistfully from our eastern casement for the first streaks of the rising dawn. It kindles in us strong desires for the day of happy meeting in our Father's house, when we shall clasp inseparable hands and climb in company the everlasting hills. Meanwhile it bids us give our hearts to Jesus only. It does for us what the departure of the two strangers from heaven did to the disciples on the Mount of Transfiguration—it leaves us alone with Jesus. It turns into deep experience that longing for home contained in the apostle's words, "having a desire to depart and to be with Christ which is far better."

The more that bereavement transforms earth into a desert, the more are our desires drawn up to heaven. Our treasures having been transferred to heaven, our hearts must follow them. Earth's hopes are smitten, and we are taught to look for "that blessed hope, the glorious appearing of the great God and our Saviour Jesus Christ." The night is falling and the flowers are folding up; but as they do so they bid us look upward and see star after star appearing upon the darkening sky.

3. *Adversity.* This may be the loss of substance, or it may be the loss of our good name, or it may be the falling away

of friends, or it may be the wrath of enemies, or it may be the disappointment of our hopes; these are what is meant by adversity. But let Job tell us what it means. "Behold, he breaketh down, and it cannot be built again, he shutteth up a man, and there can be no opening" (Job 12:14). "He hath made me weary: thou hast made desolate all my company.... I was at ease, but he hath broken me asunder: he hath also taken me by my neck, and shaken me to pieces, and set me up for his mark; his archers compass me round about, he cleaveth my reins asunder, and doth not spare;...he breaketh me with breach upon breach, he runneth upon me like a giant.... My face is foul with weeping, and on my eyelids is the shadow of death" (Job 16:7, 12, 13, 14, 16). "My days are past, my purposes are broken off, even the thoughts of my heart" (Job 17:11). "He hath fenced up my way that I cannot pass, and he hath set darkness in my paths; he hath stripped me of my glory and taken the crown from my head; he hath destroyed me on every side, and I am gone: and mine hope hath he removed like a tree...He hath put my brethren far from me, and mine acquaintance are verily estranged from me" (Job 19:8–10, 13). These are some of the drops in the bitter cup of adversity that was given to that patient saint to drink. And they are recorded for our use, on whom the ends of the world have come, and to whom these last days may perhaps fill a cup as bitter and protracted as his.

Yet let us count it all joy when we fall into divers tribulations, knowing this, that the trying of our faith worketh patience: but "let patience have her perfect work, that ye may be perfect and entire, wanting nothing" (James 1:2–4). We are cast into poverty, but how can we be poor so long as Christ is rich; and is not this poverty sent to make us prize His unsearchable riches and to buy of Him the gold tried in the fire that we may be rich? Our good name is lost through slander and false accusation. The finger of public scorn is perhaps pointed at us, and wicked men are exalted over us, triumphing in our reproach. Yet have we not the approving eye of God, and is it not enough if He still honors us and knows our innocence? Let our good name go if God sees fit thus to humble us. We have the "white stone, and in the stone a new name written, which no man knoweth save he that receiveth it" (Rev. 2:17). Friends fall off and enemies arise: false brethren turn against us, and we are doomed to bear the revilings and persecutions of those whom we have never wronged but ever loved. But the friendship of Jesus is still ours. No earthly disaster or persecutor can ever rob us of that. Nay, the coldness of those we counted on as tried and true only draws us the closer to Him, the warmth of whose love knows no abatement nor end. Joseph passed thoroughly this trial, and the Lord set him upon Pharaoh's throne.

Moses passed through it and became "king in Jeshurun." Job passed through it and was blessed a thousandfold. Daniel passed through it and was exalted with double honor. Let us "take...the prophets, who have spoken in the name of the Lord, for an example of suffering affliction, and of patience. Behold, we count them happy which endure. Ye have heard of the patience of Job, and have seen the end of the Lord; that the Lord is very pitiful, and of tender mercy" (James 5:10, 11).

Oftentimes nothing but adversity will do for us. "I spake unto thee in thy prosperity; but thou saidst, I will not hear. This hath been thy manner from thy youth, that thou obeyedst not my voice" (Jer. 22:21). We need to be stripped of every earthly portion that we may seek entirely our portion in Jehovah Himself. We need to be turned out of a home on earth that we may seek a home in heaven. Earth's music is too seducing and takes away our relish for the new song. God must either hush it or take us apart into a desert place that we may no longer be led captive by it but may have our ear open only to the heavenly melody. We cannot be trusted with too full a cup, or too pleasant a resting-place. We abuse everything that

God has given us, and prove ourselves not trustworthy as to any one of them. Some God cannot trust with health; they need sickness to keep them low and make them walk softly all their days. They need spare diet, lest the flesh should get the mastery. Others He cannot trust with prosperity; they need adversity to humble them, lest, like Jeshurun, they should wax "fat and kick." Others He cannot trust with riches; they must be kept poor, lest covetousness should spring up and pierce them through with many sorrows. Others He cannot trust with friends; they make idols of them, they give their hearts to them; and this interferes with the claims of Jehovah to have us altogether as His own.

But still in all this God dealeth with us as with the members of His own family. Never for a moment does He lose sight of this. Neither should we. So that when these things overtake us, when we are thus "judged," we should feel that we are "chastened of the Lord, that we should not be condemned with the world"; we should learn not merely to submit to the rod, but to kiss and welcome it, not merely to acquiesce in chastisement, but to "glory in tribulation, knowing that tribulation worketh patience, and patience experience, and experience hope, and hope maketh not ashamed." We should learn not merely to praise God in affliction, but to praise Him for it. We should see that the lot of the afflicted is far more enviable than that of him who is "let alone"; and, instead of trembling when we see the dark cloud of sorrow coming over us, we should tremble far more when we see it passing off, lest, perchance, that which came charged with blessing to us, should, through our stoutheartedness and unteachableness, leave us callous and unblessed.

6

The Types

The ordinance in Israel concerning the meat-offering of the firstfruits was of a very peculiar kind. Thus it was commanded, "If thou offer a meat-offering of thy firstfruits unto the Lord, thou shalt offer for the meat-offering of thy firstfruits, green ears of corn dried by the fire" (Lev. 2:14).

Christ is, we know, preeminently the firstfruits. It is He, then, who is specially prefigured by these green ears of corn dried by the fire. In this "corn" we discern the type of one who belongs to earth, partaker of our very nature. It springs up in our fields, it is nourished by our soil, it is watered by our showers, it is ripened by our sun. So was it with Jesus. He was truly Man, one of us, "the Word made flesh," the Man who "drank of the brook by the way." This corn was to be plucked when green and then dried by the fire, not in the ordinary gradual way by the heat of the sun. It was to be prematurely ripened by what we would call unnatural means, the exposure to artificial heat. In this also we see Jesus, the Man of sorrows, subjected to the Father's wrath, the wrath of Him who is a consuming fire, and withered into ripeness before His time. He did not come to His grave "in a full age, like a shock of corn in its season" (Job 5:26). He did not grow up to manhood in the calm, refreshing sunshine of Jehovah's smile.

He was scorched with fiery heat, within and without, till

age appeared upon His much-marred visage, while as yet the greenness of His strength was upon Him, so that the Jews, looking upon His wasted form, spoke of Him as one who had well-nigh reached his fiftieth year (John 8:57). Such is the view He gives of Himself in the Book of Psalms. In these we at once recognize the "green ears of corn dried by the fire." For thus He speaks, "My strength is dried up like a potsherd; and my tongue cleaveth to my jaws; and thou hast brought me unto the dust of death" (Ps. 22:15). Again, He says, "Mine eye is consumed with grief, yea, my soul and my belly; for my life is spent with grief, and my years with sighing: my strength faileth...my bones are consumed" (Ps. 31:9). Again, we hear Him saying, "Mine eye is consumed because of grief; it waxeth old because of all mine enemies" (Ps. 6:7). Such, then, was Jesus: withered and dried up before His time by reason of the sorrow which He endured for us.

But these green ears dried up by the fire are no less a description of the saints than of their Lord. Certainly they apply to Him in a way such as they never can apply to us. Yet they do stand forth as a type of the whole church, who are also called like Jesus, "the firstfruits." All the members of His body from the beginning have been just such as these dried ears of green corn. Hear, for instance, one of them speaking, "I am like a bottle in the smoke"; or again, "My bones waxed old through my roaring all the day long...my moisture is turned into the drought of summer" (Ps. 32:3, 4).

By such an emblem as this was the church's career of tribulation set before Israel. And it is most interesting for us to look at our trials in the light of so expressive a figure. Their object is to ripen us: it may be before the time; it may be in a way such as the flesh shrinks from; but still their object is to ripen us. The sorrows that compass us about are all ripening our graces, as well as withering out of us the green, rank, unripe luxuriance of earth. The heat may be great, but it shall not consume us; it will only make the ripening process a speedier one. It will shorten the way to perfect holiness and eternal glory; and shall we shrink from that which makes the process shorter?

But there was another ordinance in Israel setting forth the tribulation of the church. The mercy seat and the cherubim were to be both made of pure gold, "of beaten work" (Ex. 25:17, 18). Now, as the cherubim were doubtless the symbols of redeemed men, the church of Christ, this type is very striking. Both the mercy seat and the cherubim were to be of one piece, for "both he who sanctifieth and they who are sanctified are all of one." They are of pure gold, and this denotes their exceeding preciousness. They are made of "beaten gold," to intimate the process through which they both had passed. The mercy seat was fashioned into shape and made after the pattern showed in the mount by the stroke of the hammer. So Jesus was "made perfect through suffering." In like manner the cherubim were to be beaten into the intended shape and model. So with the saints. It is through this process that they must pass, and it is thus they are brought into that perfect shape which God has designed for them.

What, then, is the process through which the saints are passing now but just this? They are now under the hammer of the Spirit, that by this they may be fashioned into the likeness of cherubim, which in the Book of Revelation are set before us as the upbearers of Jehovah's throne and glory, as well as the inheritors thereof. And what is all the "beating" to which we may be subjected when compared with the glory for which it is preparing us? There is another figure used by our Lord in speaking of His church. He compares her to an injured, afflicted, friendless widow. Widowhood, then, is properly the church's condition here; and this is her grief. Her Lord is absent, and His absence is one of her bitterest trials. It forms one long-continued sorrow. It makes such a blank on earth that we feel as if this of itself were grief enough, even were there none besides. And were the church to realize fully her estate of widowhood, until the Lord come, she would find in this, no doubt, a new grief to which she was blind before, but a grief which operates with most blessed efficacy in sanctifying her and in keeping her apart from the world.

She is a stranger in a land of strangers. She is lonely and unfriended, sitting apart from earthly joy and fellowship. He whom she loves is far away. This separation is, as a saint of old expresses it, "like a mountain of iron upon her heavy heart." She longs to be with Him. She sighs for the day of meeting. And all this though sad is both sanctifying and solemnizing. It is a daily burden, a continual chastening, yet it is well. It loosens from earth. It lifts up to heaven. It makes the world less fascinating. It prepares for the inseparable union: the meeting time—the bridal day.

There are other figures given us of the suffering church. But let these suffice. They will help us to understand our true condition and to expect nothing else than tribulation here. No strange thing is happening to us. It is no strange thing that the green ears of corn should be dried with fire.

It is no strange thing that the cherubim should be made of beaten gold. It is no strange thing that, in the absence of the Bridegroom, the bride should mourn.

7

The Proving

There are no beings about whom we make so many mistakes as our own selves. "The heart is deceitful above all things," and besides this, the "deceitfulness of sin" is unsearchable. So that when the deceitfulness of our heart and the deceitfulness of sin come together, we need not wonder that the effect should be ignorance of ourselves.

Besides, we are unwilling to search. We shrink from the exposure which such a scrutiny would make. No doubt the consciousness of being forgiven takes away much of this reluctance. We are not so unwilling to know the worst when we are assured that however hideous the pollution thus dragged to light, it can never come between us and God. For with God all is peace. The blood that sprinkles us has made it a simple impossibility for God ever to be angry with us again. So that we come to realize in some degree the blessedness of the man whose transgression is forgiven; our spirit is "without guile." We have no object now in concealing anything from God or ourselves. We become open, frank, straightforward. Still the search is a painful one, and we would rather postpone it. It might bring many things to light which would shock and humble us. It might alarm us with the extent of the evil which still remains in us, even though it could not bring us into condemnation. Hence, we are slow to learn, or even to inquire into, the evil that cleaves to us still.

Moreover, we are not at all persuaded that there is so very much evil in us. We do not know ourselves. Our convictions of sin have been but shallow, and we are beginning to imagine that the conflict between the flesh and the spirit is not so very fierce and deadly as we had conceived it to be. We think we have rid ourselves of many of our sins entirely, and are in a fair way speedily getting rid of all the rest. The depths of sin in us we have never sounded; the number of our abominations we have never thought of marking. We have been sailing smoothly to the kingdom, and perhaps at times were wondering how our lot should be so different from the saints of old. We thought, too, that we had overcome many of our corruptions. The old man was crucified. It seemed dead, or at least feigned itself to be so in order to deceive us. Our lusts had abated. Our tempers had improved. Our souls were calm and equable. Our mountain stood strong, and we were saying, "We shall never be moved." The victory over self and sin seemed, in some measure, won. Alas, we were blind! We were profoundly ignorant of our hearts.

Well, the trial came. It swept over us like a cloud of the night, or rather through us like an icy blast, piercing and chilling us to the vitals. Then the old man within us awoke, and, as if in response to the uproar without, a fiercer tempest broke loose within. We felt as if the four winds of heaven had been let loose to strive together upon the great deep within us. Unbelief arose in its former strength. Rebelliousness raged in every region of our soul. Unsubdued passions resumed their strength. We were utterly dismayed at the fearful scene. But yesterday this seemed impossible. Alas, we know not the strength of sin nor the evil of our hearts till God thus allowed them to break loose.

It was thus He dealt with Israel; and for this end He led them into the desert. "The Lord thy God led thee these forty years in the wilderness, to humble thee, and to prove thee, to know what was in thine heart" (Deut. 8:2). Their desert trials put them to the proof. And when thus proved, what iniquity was found in them! What sin came out which had lain hidden and unknown before! The trial did not create the evil: it merely brought out what was there already, unnoticed and unfelt, like a torpid adder. Then the heart's deep fountains were broken up, and streams of pollution came rushing out, black as hell. Rebellion, unbelief, fretfulness, atheism, idolatry, self-will, self-confidence, self-pleasing—all burst out when the blast of the desert met them in the face and called Egypt to remembrance with its luxurious plenty. Thus they were proved. Even so it is with the saints still. God chastens them that He may draw forth the evil that is lying concealed and unsuspected within. The rod smites us on the tenderest part, and we start up in a moment as if in arms against God. The flesh, the old man, is cut to the quick, and forthwith arouses itself, displaying all of a sudden much of its former strength. When it was asleep we did not know its power, but now that it has been awakened, its remains of strength appall us.

It is not till the sea is "troubled," that "its waters cast up mire and dirt." When all was calm, there seemed naught but purity pervading it, and ripple folded over ripple in the still brightness of its transparent green. But the winds break loose, the tempest stirs its lowest depths, and then all is changed. Thus we see it in the saints. When calamity breaks over them like a tempest, then the hidden evils of their hearts awaken. Sins scarcely known before display themselves. The heart pours out its wickedness. Hard thoughts of God arise. Atheistical murmurings break out and refuse to be restrained.

Questionings both of His wisdom and of His love are muttered; yea, how often do they assume a more explicit form, and we ask, "If God be so loving and wise, why is it thus?" We could not have expected such treatment at His hands. Distrust and unbelief assume the mastery, and we refuse to acquiesce to His will. It seems hard to be smitten so severely and laid so low. For a while it seems as if the heart were determined to think evil thoughts of God and never to think well of Him again. And, though a calm ensues and we become both ashamed and terrified at our rebelliousness, still the heart has given forth its pollution. We have learned its unsearchable depths of evil. We are led, on the one hand, into deeper views of our own amazing and incredible vileness; and on the other, into fuller discoveries of the abounding grace of God. We learn to prize more the open fountain, and we betake ourselves anew for covering to the righteousness of the Righteous One.

It is remarkable that when the saints of old were tried and proved, there was found in them not only evil but the very evil we should least of all have anticipated. We should have said of Noah, for instance, that he was one whose sobriety and self-restraint would be carried with him to his grave. He stood alone amid a luxurious, sensual, intoxicated world, condemning their lasciviousness and revelry. Yet no sooner is he placed in circumstances of temptation than he falls. Noah becomes drunken!

Again, Abraham stands out preeminent for faith and courage; yet, when he goes to Egypt and Gerar, his faith gives way, and he utters lies through fear. Lot had withstood all the sensuality and filthiness of Sodom, and his righteous soul mourned over their abominations; yet, scarce is he delivered from the city's destruction than he falls into drunkenness and lust equal to that of the cities that had been consumed. Job, though marked for his patience, gave way to impatience in the day of trial. Moses, the meekest of all men, displayed his anger and "spake unadvisedly with his lips." David was one of the bravest that ever fought the battles of the Lord in Israel, and he had gone out against Goliath with a sling and a stone, yet when he fled before Saul and came to King Achish at Gath, his courage was gone, and he feigned himself a madman through fear of his enemies. Elijah had stood before kings without trembling to pronounce the sentence of judgment, to shut up the heavens, and to wield the sword of Jehovah's vengeance, though alone amid tens of thousands. Yet he flees before a woman's threat; he gives up all for lost and requests to die.

Ezekiel, whose character shines out as one of singular holiness and obedience, yet records against himself a strange instance of unsubmissiveness, when sent by God on an errand of judgment to Israel: "I went in bitterness, in the heat [marg. hot anger] of my spirit; but the hand of the Lord was strong upon me (Ezek. 3:14). Peter's attachment to his Lord is one of his peculiar characteristics, yet it was Peter who denied Him. John was the disciple who seems to have been most like his Master in gentleness and love, yet it was John who wanted to call down fire from heaven upon the Samaritan village.

Lord, what is man! And what is a human heart—the heart even of thy saints when proved and held up to view? "O heart, heart," said John Berridge of himself, "what art thou? A mass of fooleries and absurdities, the vainest, wickedest, craftiest, foolishest thing in nature." What deep-hidden evil, what selfishness, what pride, what harsh tempers, what worldliness come out in a moment, when the stroke goes deep into the soul! How long Job remained steadfast, holding fast his integrity and confidence in God! Stroke after stroke laid him prostrate, yet he gave glory to God in the midst of desolation and sorrow. The inner circle of self had not been reached. But when a loathsome disease drove him to the dunghill, and his friends rose up against him and addressed him as a man marked out by God as guilty, then his faith and patience gave way. The very center of his being had been reached and probed; and forth came the stream of impatience and unbelief. It takes a sharp arrow and a strongly drawn bow to pierce into the inmost circle; yet

God in kindness spares not. The seat of the disease must be reached, and its real nature brought out to the light.

Of all the evils which are thus drawn forth from the heart of the saint, the worst, and yet the commonest, are hard thoughts of God. Yet who would have expected this? Once, indeed, in our unbelieving days our souls were full of these. Our thoughts of God were all evil together. When the Holy Spirit wrought in our hearts the mighty change, the special thing which He accomplished was teaching us to think well of God, showing us how little He had deserved these hard thoughts from us, how much He had deserved the opposite. The wondrous tale of manifold love, which the gospel brought to us, won our hearts and made us ashamed of our distrust. We said then, Surely we shall never think ill of God again. "Though he slay me, yet will I trust in him." We thought that affliction would only make us cleave to Him the more. Yet scarcely does He begin to smite us than our former thoughts return. We wonder why He should treat us thus. We suspect His love and faithfulness. Our hold of His grace seems to loosen, as if at times it would wholly give way.

We are like Jonah with his withered gourd. We think we do well to be angry even unto death. God does not seem the same loving God as when first we believed and tasted forgiveness from His gracious hands. Alas, the treachery of our hearts has been at length discovered. We find that we were not serving God for naught. May He not expostulate with us and ask us, "Doest thou well to be angry?" Would not this question close our lips forever? Doest thou well to be angry or desponding, when God hath forgiven all thine iniquities and removed them from thee, as far as the East is from the West? Doest thou well to be angry when thou art delivered from the wrath to come, as well as from a present evil world, and safely lodged within the clefts of the rock with Jesus as thy companion there? Doest thou well to be angry when the Father's love is thine assured portion, and the kingdom of the Son thine inheritance forever? Doest thou well to be angry when the night is far spent and the day is at hand, when the distant eastern clouds are taking on their rosy fringes, and the daystar is preparing to arise?[1]

---

1. God's chastened ones will find many precious words of counsel and consolation in Samuel Rutherford's letters. Having been tried, he knew how to speak a word in season to the weary. Hear some of them, "I wonder many times that ever a child of God should have a sad heart, considering what the Lord is preparing for him." "When we shall come home, and enter into the possession of our brother's fair kingdom, and when our heads shall find the weight of the eternal crown of glory, and when we shall look back to pains and sufferings, then shall we see life and sorrow to be less than one step or stride from a prison to a glory, and that our little inch of time-suffering is not worthy of our first night's welcome home to heaven." "However matters go, the worst shall be a tired traveler, and a joyful and sweet welcome home."

8

The Rebuking

It is worthwhile noticing the word which is used in the two well-known passages which speak of chastisement, "Nor faint when thou art rebuked of him" (Heb. 12:5). "As many as I love, I rebuke and chasten" (Rev. 3:19). A little inquiry into its meaning and a little comparing of texts will help to set it in its true light. It is the same word used in Matthew 18:15: "If thy brother shall trespass against thee, go and tell him his fault." It is the same word used in Luke 3:19, when John is said to have reproved Herod. It is the same word used in John 16:8, "When he is come, he will reprove the world of sin." We learn, then, from these expressions, that rebuke is not simply some stern word or frown, implying displeasure on the part of God, but such a frown which "tells us our faults"—such a frown which reproves or convicts us of sin. It is God's way of pointing out what He sees to be amiss in us, of calling our attention to it as a thing which displeases Him, and, on account of which, if not put away, He must certainly deal with us in chastisement.

The word "rebuke" seems to imply something more gentle than chastisement. And it is of some importance to consider it in this light. I know not a better illustration of it than Christ's address to the churches of Asia. The especial preciousness of these lies in this that they show us what the heart of Christ is when reproving. What a discovery do they give us of this! Let us hear Him addressing them. Thus He rebukes the angel of the church of Ephesus: "Nevertheless I have somewhat against thee, because thou hast left thy first love; remember therefore from whence thou art fallen, and repent." Thus He rebukes the church of Pergamos: "I have a few things against thee, because thou hast there them that hold the doctrine of Balaam...repent, or else I will come unto thee quickly, and will fight against thee with the sword of my mouth." In like manner we might quote His other rebukes to the other churches as illustrations of our meaning. But these are enough. They show the gentleness of the Reprover both in the manner and the language. They are faithful, indeed, but how delicate, how tender, how mild! They point out what is amiss with all distinctness and directness, yet in a manner the most fitted to win and in language the least likely to offend. He begins each of them by making most gracious mention of the past services and excellent deeds of the angel of the church, as if desirous to show how willing He was to praise, insofar as He could, and how unwilling to blame, save when it could not be avoided. In listening to this voice speaking from heaven, we seem to hear the same meek and lowly One that once spake on earth in the house of Simon the Pharisee. Wishing to reprove him for his evil thoughts of the woman who stood behind the Lord and washed His feet with her tears, He began thus mildly His rebuke, "Simon, I have somewhat to say unto thee."

Yet while the rebuke of God is thus mild and loving, it is both faithful and solemn. It is faithful, for it hides nothing from us. Its tone is soft, yet the words are full of meaning. They are quite explicit in their condemnation of the sin perceived in us. And the rebuke of Jehovah is a solemn thing; not the rebuke of wrath, for that has passed away, yet it makes us stand in awe. The rebuke of love is as solemn a thing as the rebuke of wrath. A parent's rebuke is much to a loving child; how much more is the rebuke of our God—the God who made heaven and earth!

Many are the rebukes which He administers. Some of them are lighter and others heavier. Yet in both He is laying His finger upon sin and intimating distinctly His desire that we should turn from it. To the former kind I fear we oftentimes give but little heed. The touch of transient pain, a brief illness, a slight indisposition, a passing weakness, some common domestic vexation, some trivial casualty, some few days parting from one we love, some unkind word where least we looked for it, some disappointment or annoyance— these are all fatherly rebukes of the lighter and gentler kind. They are not so sharp as many others, yet they are not the less on that account the indications of a father's will. They are apt to be overlooked, for they are slighter and commoner than many and do not force themselves upon our notice. Yet surely it is worth our while to point them out and to make them the subject of special and prolonged consideration.

It is difficult to understand why we should so much undervalue them. To one who weighs them aright, they cannot but seem peculiarly precious and affecting. Their frequency makes us familiar with them, and on this account we slight them. Sad and strange! Does not their frequency show the unwearied pains that God is taking with us, giving us precept upon precept, line upon line? Should that very thing in them which displays God's untiring earnestness, His assiduous vigilance, and intense anxiety for our welfare tempt us to disregard such dealings? Their mildness, also, as well as their frequency, tends to make us undervalue them. Unaccountable perversity! They are so slight and so gentle; therefore, they are not to be owned as the laying on of a father's hand! Had they been sharper and heavier they would have been recognized as such, but being so tender they are hardly worthy of our serious notice!

On this point I am persuaded that an admonition is much

needed, not merely by a heedless world, but even by the saints of God. The point adverted to is a much neglected one, and yet it is one which every day's events press upon our notice. A raging fever prostrates us. Our strength gives way. Our life is despaired of. Then we say, "This is the finger of God. This is His rebuke." But we take a slight cold, or sustain some slight injury—there is no danger and perhaps no piercing pain—then, alas! we do not own the doing of God; or, at the most, we own it vaguely and carelessly. The gentleness of the infliction makes us feel at liberty to undervalue it, and to forget it as coming from God. Ah! it is thus that we "despise his chastenings."

And what is the consequence? We draw upon ourselves severer chastisement. We provoke God to visit us with heavier blows. We compel Him to chastise by our heedlessness of His rebuke. We make bitter trial absolutely necessary.

Let us never forget this. It is our own frowardness and negligence that impose a necessity for the infliction of suffering. Affliction is not a desirable thing in itself. It would be better could it be avoided. God afflicts not willingly. But we constrain Him. Many a sorrow we might escape were we not so heedless and unbelieving. Most slowly and reluctantly does God stretch out His hand to chasten. For a while He wounds most slightly and mildly. If we may speak after the manner of men, He just hints or whispers His reproof. He is most unwilling to employ sharpness. He tarries long. He lingers on His way to smite. He tries other means. He sends milder trials first that we may be led to self-searching and repentance and that He may be spared the necessity of inflicting a heavier blow. But we trifle with these; and then, at last, He lifts up His voice and speaks in a way which can neither be overlooked nor mistaken. How sad that we should thus so stubbornly persist in filling the cup of sorrow which God would fain have spared us! Let us open our ears to the rebuke of God. His "still small voice" should be as effectual as the lightning or the earthquake. Let us learn the meaning and use of slighter trials. Let us count no touch of pain or grief, however mild or transient, too insignificant for our most serious thought. This would save us much. It would teach us many a blessed lesson in an easy, pleasant way. Every trouble, however light, comes fragrant with blessing. Shall we then overlook it or thrust it away? It is a new opportunity of getting nearer God and learning more of His love. How foolish, how sinful, to disregard it! God is saying to us, "Improve this light cross, and you will not need a heavier." But we are deaf. And, oh, how much this deafness costs us!

It is not, however, our deafness under light troubles only that draws on us the heavier. We are too heedless even of these heavier ones, and this prepares for us heavier still. The easy way in which some get over trials is very sad. There is a vehement outburst of feeling at the moment; and occasionally there may be a recurrence of this for some time after the calamity has spent itself, but, with the exception of such fits of grief, there is nothing like laying the trial to heart. To lay a visitation solemnly to heart is something very different from indulging in wild bursts of grief. Hence, it will generally be found that those who give way to these are often, during the intervals between them, very easy and mirthful. This unequal pressure of trial is not only in itself injurious to the soul, but it neutralizes the right influence of trial, and thus renders necessary another and more stunning blow.

Hence, it is that we so often observe that when God takes up a case in earnest, if anyone may so speak, it is either by a succession of strokes, following each other closely, or else by a long protracted sorrow. And it is we who procure these things unto ourselves, in that we have forsaken the Lord our God, when He led us by the way (Jer. 2:17). Billow after billow breaks over us, but we ourselves have called forth the storm; and it is our perversity that is keeping it alive, nay, perhaps, raising the surges higher till we are well-nigh overwhelmed.

Had we but yielded to God at once, and allowed Him to bless us as He desired, one wave might have been enough, and ere evening the storm breeze might have died away. Yet, even in this there is consolation. Our foolishness is making our voyage a rough one, but it is homeward bound. All these many blasts and billows are toward Canaan, not away from it; and sometimes, from their topmost crest, we get a brighter glimpse of our eternal heritage than from the level calm of more unruffled days. It brightens the blackness of the tempest, and disarms it of many a terror to know that each blast, however fierce, is bearing us homeward, that each billow, however rough, is carrying us more swiftly to our desired haven.

9

The Purifying

Chastisement supposes sin. Suffering does not, for Jesus suffered, nay, "learned obedience by the things which he suffered," but chastisement does. Some have, indeed, applied the word chastisement to Jesus also, for He was "made perfect through suffering," and in the sense of passing through discipline that He might know by experience our condition here and be seen as the doer of the Father's will, the Man that "pleased not himself"—in this sense His sorrows might be called by that name, yet in no other. For although tempted in all points like as we are, He was without sin. But in our case it is altogether different. It is sin in us that draws down the infliction, just as the rod attracts the lightning from the clouds.

Yet it is all forgiven sin. In looking to the cross we found forgiveness. As believers in Jesus, we "have no more conscience of sin." Still the flesh remains. The old man is ever at work within us. "Iniquities prevail against us"; and though we know that they are purged away, still they cleave to us. Our nature is still defiled though our conscience has been cleansed. It is against sin still existing within us, though forgiven, that chastisement is directed. The casting of gold or silver into the furnace implies that there is dross upon them that requires to be purged out with fire. Were there no dross, there would be no need for furnace or fire or refiner's labor. These are but means of getting rid of the dross. The fire which the Lord is to kindle in the earth, when He comes again, proves that sin is found upon it. Were there no curse lying on the earth no purifying fire would be needed. But the blight must be burned out, the trail of the serpent must be swept clean away; and therefore the earth must be cast into the furnace that out of it may come a new and more glorious creation, fit for God to look upon, and for holy men to dwell in, and from which, therefore, every trace of corruption must be totally erased.

So with chastisement. It has reference to sin. Were it not for sin, chastisement would be unknown. In heaven there is no chastisement, for there is no sin. Angels know nothing of it, for they know no sin. They see it afar off; they hear the sad story of earth. They witness the tribulations of the church, but that is all. For it is only where there is sin that there is chastisement. Its existence here is just God's voice, saying, "I have found iniquity upon the earth." Its infliction on an individual is God saying, "I have seen sin on thee." I do not take up the question as to particular trials being the result of particular sins in individuals. In many cases we know that this is the case. In others it is more doubtful. And hence, though it is well in affliction to ask what special sin or sins God is pointing at, it is wrong in us to fix exclusively upon one or two instead of turning our attention to the whole body of sin and directing our efforts against that.

But chastisement supposes also a determination on the part of God to get rid of sin. It is the expression of His hatred of it, and of His settled purpose to deliver from it. To purify us is what He seeks; and this He is resolved to accomplish at whatever cost. It must be done, for He cannot look upon iniquity. And what is pain if it expels sin? What is sorrow, if it helps to purge away the evil of our nature—a lifetime of accumulated dross?

There are several figures which God employs for pointing out His designs in chastising us. Let us enumerate these:

1. *It is a refining.* The saints are "chosen in the furnace of affliction" (Isa. 48:10), and "when he hath tried me, I shall come forth as gold" (Job 23:10). The heat of the furnace burns out the dross and leaves the pure metal behind. It is in the furnace that the flesh is destroyed and the old man gets his death-stroke. It is in the furnace that self-confidence is uptorn, unbelief is broken, and faith is strengthened and purified. Were it not for the furnace, what would become of our dross and alloy? And then when the silver is in the crucible, the Refiner Himself comes near. Hear how the Lord hath spoken concerning this: "Thus saith the Lord of hosts, Behold, I will melt them and try them, for how shall I do for the daughter of my people?" (Jer. 9:7) "I will turn my hand upon thee, and purely purge away thy dross, and take away all thy tin (Isa. 1:25). "When the Lord...shall have purged the blood of Jerusalem from the midst thereof by the spirit of judgment and by the spirit of burning" (Isa. 4:4).

2. *It is a sifting.* "Lo, I will command, and I will sift the house of Israel among all nations, like as corn is sifted in a sieve" (Amos 9:9). We are God's corn, grown in His fields and gathered in by His hand. Yet we are coarse and rough grain. Many a sifting process we must pass through in order to separate the coarser particles that nothing but the finest may remain. Affliction sifts us. Persecution sifts us. God has many a sieve, some finer and some coarser, and He makes us to pass through them according as we require. He sifts the professing church, and many fall off. He applies a finer sieve, and many more fall off. He takes each church by itself, each congregation by itself, and sifts them, and many false brethren are discovered. He takes each believer and sifts him individually and his coarser particles pass off. This process is repeated. He is winnowed and sifted again and again till the grain is purified.

3. *It is a pruning.* "Every branch that beareth fruit, he purgeth it, that it may bring forth more fruit" (John 15:2). We are the branches of the vine. Christ is the Father's vine: the stem and root of all spiritual life. Over this precious vine the Father watches. His desire is that "the branch of the Lord should be beautiful and glorious," that this vine should yield its fruit in its season. Hence, He not only waters it, but keeps it night and day. And He prunes it with the skill and care of a husbandman. He wishes to make each branch fruitful as well as comely, and He spares no pains, for "herein is he glorified if we bear much fruit." How much we owe to this heavenly pruning! What rank, luxuriant branches does it cut away! What earthliness, what foolishness, what waywardness, what hastiness, what fleshly lusts, what selfish narrowness are all, one by one, skillfully pruned away by the vine-dresser's careful knife!

4. *It is a polishing.* We are "living stones," placed one by one, upon the great foundation stone laid in Zion for the heavenly temple. These stones must first be quarried out of the mass. This the Holy Spirit does at conversion.

Then, when cut out, the hewing and squaring begin. And God uses affliction as His hammer and chisel for accomplishing this. Many a stroke is needed; and after being thus hewn into shape, the polishing goes on. All roughness must be smoothed away. The stone must be turned around and around on every side that no part of it may be left unpolished.

The temple indeed is above, and we are below. But this is God's design. As the stones of Solomon's temple were all to be prepared at a distance and then brought to Jerusalem, there to be built together, so the living stones of the heavenly temple are all made ready here to be fitted in without the noise of an axe or hammer into the glorious building not made with hands. Everyone then must be polished here; and while there are many ways of doing this, the most effectual is suffering. And this is God's design in chastisement. This is what the Holy Spirit effects: as like a workman He stands over each stone, touching and retouching it, turning it on every side, marking its blemishes and roughness, and then applying His tools to effect the desired shape and polish. Some parts of the stone are so rugged and hard that nothing save heavy and repeated strokes and touches will smooth them down. They resist every milder treatment. And yet, in patient love, this heavenly Workman carries on the Father's purpose concerning us. Keeping beside Him, if one may thus speak after the manner of men, the perfect Model according to which the stone is to be fashioned—even Jesus, the Father's chosen One—He labors till every part is shaped according to His likeness, line after line. No pains are spared, no watchfulness relaxed, till we are made entirely like Him, being changed into the same image from glory to glory by the Spirit of the Lord.

Thus affliction molds and purifies. Thus it effaces the resemblance of the first Adam and traces in us each lineament of the second that "as we have borne the image of the earthly, we may also bear the image of the heavenly." "Oh," said a saint of other days, "what I owe to the file, to the hammer, to the furnace of my Lord Jesus!" Come, then, let us question ourselves and endeavor to ascertain what affliction has been doing for us and what progress we are making in putting off the old man and in putting on the new. Am I loving my worldliness of spirit and becoming heavenly minded? Am I getting rid of my pride, my passion, my stubbornness, and becoming humble, mild, and teachable? Are all my idols displaced and broken, and do I use my creature comforts as though I used them not? Am I caring less for the honors of time, for man's love, man's smile, man's applause? Am I crucified to the world and is the world crucified to me by the cross of Christ; or am I still ashamed of His reproach, and am I half-reluctant to follow Him through bad report and through good, through honor and through shame? Do I count it my glory and my joy to walk where He has led the way, to suffer wherein He suffered, to drink of the cup of which He drank, and to be baptized with the baptism wherewith He was baptized? Or, while professing to seek the kingdom hereafter, do I refuse to undergo that tribulation through which I must enter; while willing to secure the crown of glory, do I shrink back from the crown of thorns? Am I every day becoming more and more unlike the children of earth, more and more fashioned after the likeness, and bearing the special lineaments, of my Elder Brother, of whom the whole family in Heaven and earth is named? Do I realize this earth as neither my portion nor my rest, and, knowing that one chain may bind me as fast to the world as a thousand, am I careful to shake off every fetter that may bind me to the vanities of a world like this? Is chastisement really purifying me? Am I conscious of its blessed effects upon my soul? Can I look back upon such and such scenes of trial and say, "There and then I learned most precious lessons; there and then I got rid of some of the body of this death; there and then I got up to a higher level from which I am striving to ascend to one higher still?" Have I learned much of the sympathy of Jesus and known the blessedness of having such an One as He to weep along with me in my day of sorrow? Have I wiped off my rebellious tears and been taught to shed only those of love and submissive fondness, tears of brotherhood and sympathy, tears of longing to be absent from the body and present with the Lord?

To make us "partakers of his holiness" is God's great design as stated by the apostle. And there is something very remarkable about the expression. It corresponds to a similar one in the Second Epistle of Peter, "partakers of the divine nature." It implies something very exalted and very blessed; much more so than if it had merely been told us that God's aim was to "make us holy." Partakers of His own very holiness—His very nature! This is more than angels can glory in. It is something peculiar to "the redeemed from among men"—the members of the Body of Christ. And it is in this way that Jesus speaks to us. It is not merely "peace" that He promises to us, but His own peace—"my peace." It is not merely joy He bestows; but His own joy—"my joy." So here it is not merely holiness He is conferring upon us, but His own holiness. His wish is to make us partakers of that. And oh, how much does that imply!

A goodly prize this—one for the obtaining of which we may well count all things but loss! It is well for us when we come to see it in all its value and excellency and to set our hearts upon it. Until we do so there will be strife between us and God, for this is the blessing which above all others He desires for us and which He is bent on conferring upon us. When, however, we come to be perfectly at one with Him as to this, then the struggle ceases. He gets His own way, and this is best for us. How blessed when His desire to deliver us from sin, and ours to be delivered from it, meet together; when His purpose to make us holy is cordially responded to by our fervent longings to be so! Then it is that the divine fullness flows into the soul without a check, and, notwithstanding the bitterness of the outward process by which this is effected, joy unspeakable and full of glory, possesses the consecrated soul. "Wherefore, laying aside every weight, and the sin which doth so easily beset us, let us run with patience the race set before us, looking unto Jesus, the author and the finisher of our faith, who for the joy set before him endured the cross, despising the shame." And there is nothing like affliction for teaching us this. It acts like the wind upon the trees, making them take deeper root. It is the mowing of the grass that it may shoot up thicker and greener. It is the shaking of the torch that it may blaze the brighter.

10

The Arousing

It may have been long since the Holy Spirit awoke us from our sleep of death. Into that same deep sleep we know that we shall never fall again. He who awoke us will keep us awake until Jesus comes. In that sense we shall sleep no more.

But still much of our drowsiness remains. We are not wholly awake, and oftentimes much of our former sleep returns. Dwelling on the world's enchanted ground, our eyes close, our senses are bewildered, our conscience loses its sensitiveness, and our faculties their energy; we fall asleep even upon our watchtower, forgetful that the night is far spent, and the day is at hand.

While thus asleep, or half-asleep, all goes wrong. Our movements are sluggish and lifeless. Our faith waxes feeble; our love is chilled; our zeal cools down. The freshness of other years is gone. Our boldness has forsaken us. Our schemes are carelessly devised and drowsily executed. The work of God is hindered by us instead of being helped forward. We are a drag upon it. We mar it.

But God will not have it so. Neither for His work's sake nor for His saints' sake can He suffer this to continue. We must be aroused at whatsoever cost. We are not to be allowed to sleep as do others. We must watch and be sober, for we are children of the light and of the day, not of the night nor of darkness. God cannot permit us thus to waste life, as if its only use were to be sported with or trifled away. Duties lazily and lifelessly performed; halfhearted prayers; a deportment, blameless enough perhaps, but tame and unexpressive, and therefore uninfluential; words well and wisely spoken perhaps but without weight—these are not things which God can tolerate in a saint. It is either the coldness of Sardis to which He says, "If thou shalt not watch, I will come on thee as a thief, and thou shalt not know what hour I will come upon thee." Or it is the lukewarmness of Laodicea to which He says, "Because thou art lukewarm, and neither cold nor hot, I will spew thee out of my mouth."

In arousing us God proceeds at first most gently. He touches us slightly, as the angel did Elijah under the juniper tree, that He may awaken us. He sends some slight visitation to shake us out of our security. He causes us to hear some distant noise: it may be the tumults of the nations, or it may be the tidings of famine, or war, or pestilence afar off. Perhaps this entirely fails; we slumber on as securely as ever. Our life is as listless and as useless as ever. Then He comes nearer, and makes His voice to be heard in our own neighborhood or within the circle of our kindred. This also fails. Then He comes nearer still, for the time is hurrying on and the saint is still asleep. He speaks into our very ears. He smites upon some tender part till every fiber of our frame quivers and every pulse throbs quicker. Our very soul is stricken through as with a thousand arrows. Then we start up like one awakening out of a long sleep, and, looking round us, wonder how we could have slept so long.

But oh, how difficult it is to awaken us thoroughly! It needs stroke upon stroke in long succession to do this. After every waking up there is the continual tendency to fall back again into slumber, so that we need both to be made awake and to be kept awake. What sorrows does our drowsiness cost us—what bleeding, broken hearts! The luxury of "ease in Zion" indulged in perhaps for years has been dearly bought.

"Think of living," was the pregnant maxim of the thoughtful German. "Thy life," says another, quoting the above, "wert thou the pitifulest of all the sons of earth is no idle dream, but a solemn reality. It is thy own. It is all thou hast to confront eternity with. Work then, like a star, unhasting yet unresting."

There are some Christians who work, but they do not work like men awake. They move forward in a certain track of duty, but it is with weary footstep. Their motions are constrained and cold. They do many good things, devise many good schemes, say excellent things, but the vigorous pulse of warm life is wanting. Zeal, glowing zeal—elastic and untiring—is not theirs. They neither burn themselves, no do they kindle others. There is nothing of the star about them save its coldness. They may expect some sharp stroke of chastisement, for they need it.

There are others who are only wakeful by fits and starts. They cannot be safely counted on, for their fervor depends upon the humor of the moment. A naturally impulsive temperament, of which, perhaps, they are not sufficiently aware, and which they have not sought either to crucify or to regulate, renders them uncertain in all their movements. This intermittent wakefulness effects but little. They do and they undo. They build up and they pull down. They kindle and quench the flame alternately. There is nothing of the "star" about them. They stand in need of some sore and long continued pressure to equalize the variable, fitful movements of their spirit.

There are others who seem to be always wakeful, but then it is the wakefulness of bustle and restlessness. They cannot live but in the midst of stirring, and scheming, and moving to and fro. Their temperament is that nervous, tremulous, impatient kind that makes rest or retirement to be felt as restraint and pain. These seldom effect much themselves, but they are often useful by their perpetual stir and friction for setting or keeping others in motion and preventing stagnation around them. But their incessant motion prevents their being filled with the needed grace. Their continual contact with the outward things of religion hinders their inward growth and mars their spirituality. These are certainly in one sense like the star, wakeful and unresting, but they move forward with such haste that instead of gathering light or giving it forth, they are losing every day the little that they possessed. A deep sharp stroke will be needed for shaking off this false fervor and imparting the true calm wakefulness of spirit, to which, as saints, they are called. It is the deepening of spiritual feeling that is needed in their case, and it takes much chastening to accomplish this.

There are others who are always steadily at work and apparently with fervor too. Yet a little intercourse with them shows that they are not truly awake. They work so much more than they pray that they soon become like vessels without oil. They are farther on than the last class, yet still they need arousing. They are like the star, both "unresting and unhasting," yet their light is dim. Its reflection upon a dark world is faint and pale. It is a deeper spiritual life and experience that they need; and for this, it may be there is some sore visitation in store for them.

The true wakeful life is different from all these. It is a thing of intensity and depth. It carries ever about with it the air of calm and restful dignity, of inward power and greatness. It is fervent, but not feverish; energetic, but not excited; speedy in its doings, but not hasty; prudent, but not timid or selfish; resolute and fearless, but not rash; unobtrusive and sometimes, it may be, silent, yet making all around to feel its influence; full of joy and peace, yet without parade or noise; overflowing in tenderness and love, yet at the same time, faithful and true. This is the wakeful life! But oh, before it is thoroughly attained, how much are we sometimes called upon to suffer through the rebelliousness of a carnal nature that will not let us surrender ourselves up wholly to God, and present ourselves as living sacrifices, which is our reasonable service! In thus arousing us from our slumber, chastisement not merely makes us more energetic, more laborious, but it makes us far more prayerful. Perhaps it is here that the waking up is most sensibly felt. Nothing so quickens prayer as trial. It sends us at once to our knees and shuts the door of our closet behind us. In the day of prosperity we have many comforts, many refuges to resort to; in the day of sorrow we have only one, and that is God. Our grief is too deep to tell to any other; it is too heavy for any other to soothe. Now we awake to prayer. It was something to us before, but now it is all. Man's arm fails, and there is none but God to lean upon. Our closets, in truth, are the only places of light in a world which has now become doubly dark to us. All without and around is gloom. Clouds overshadow the whole region. Only the closet is bright and calm. How eagerly, how thankfully we betake ourselves to it now! We could spend our whole time in this happy island of light which God has provided for us in the midst of a stormy ocean. When compelled at times to leave it, how gladly do we return to it! What peaceful hours of solitude we have there with God for our one companion! We can almost forget that the clouds of earth are still above us and its tempest still rioting around us. Prayer becomes a far more real thing than ever. It is prized now as it was never prized before. We cannot do without it. Of necessity, as well as of choice, we must pray, sending up our cries from the depths. It becomes a real asking, a real pleading. It is no form now. What new life, new energy, new earnestness are poured into each petition! It is the heart that is now speaking, and the lips cannot find words wherewith to give utterance to its desires. The groanings that "cannot be uttered" are all that now burst forth and ascend up into the ear of God. Formerly, there was often the lip without the heart; now it is far oftener the heart without the lip. Now we know how "the Spirit helpeth our infirmities."

We begin to feel what it is to "pray in the Holy Ghost. "There is a new nearness to God. Communion with Him is far more of a conscious reality now. It is close dealing with a living, personal Jehovah. New arguments suggest themselves; new desires spring up; new wants disclose themselves. Our own emptiness and God's manifold fullness are brought before us so vividly that the longings of our inmost souls are kindled, and our heart crieth out for God, for the living God. It was David's sorrows that quickened prayer in him. It was in the belly of the whale that Jonah was taught to cry aloud. And it was among the thorns of the wilderness and the fetters of Babylon that Manasseh learned to pray. Church of Christ— chosen heritage of the Lord—awake! Children of the light and of the day, arise! The long winter night is nearly over. The day-star is preparing to ascend. "The end of all things is at hand: be ye therefore sober, and watch unto prayer" (1 Peter 4:7). "Why sleep ye? rise and pray, lest ye enter into temptation!" (Luke 2:46).

11

The Solemnizing

Laughter and gaiety belong to a fallen world. They are too superficial to have place among the holy; and too hollow to be known among the truly happy. With the peace of God in our hearts we feel that we do not need them. They may do for childhood; they may do for the world; but not for us. They do not suit our feelings; they are not deep or solid enough to be in harmony with our new nature. They are not the utterances of a truly happy soul. Yet we live in a gay world that rings everywhere with hollow laughter. Around us are the sights and sounds of mirth by which vain men are seeking to cheat away their ever-fretting uneasiness, to soothe their ruffled consciences, or to drown their bitter sorrows. Oftentimes the saints seem to catch the tone of levity, making mirth with the most mirthful, jesting with the most foolish, singing, perhaps, the world's songs of vanity, speaking its idle words, walking in its vain paths as if its friendships and pleasures were not forbidden things.

Apart, however, from the contagion of the world's influence our tone is apt to fall low and our deportment to lose that solidity and seriousness which become the saints. Almost unconsciously and without knowing how, we get light and airy; we give way to the current of vain thoughts; we forget to set a guard upon our lips; we indulge in foolish talking and jesting in our meetings with each other. Our words are not "with grace, seasoned with salt." We forget the admonition, "Let no corrupt communication proceed out of your mouths, but that which is good to the use of edifying, that it may minister grace to the hearers." This propensity grows upon us. Seriousness becomes a thing reserved entirely for the closet or the sanctuary. We forget our character as saints, called out of darkness and "delivered from a present evil world." We lose sight of our heavenly parentage and divine adoption. Our whole habits of thought, feeling, speaking, and doing too much resemble the flippancies of a heedless, lighthearted world, whose maxim is, "let us eat, drink, and be merry."

Thus our spirituality decays. Heavenly mindedness is gone. We become of the earth, earthly. Our souls cleave to the dust, and we are content to grovel there. We become lean and barren, neither growing ourselves nor helping the growth of others. Our blossoms send forth no fragrance, our branches bear no fruit. We grieve the Holy Spirit of God whereby we are sealed unto the day of redemption. He cannot dwell with levity and mirth any more than amid profanity and crime. He retires from the temple into which He had come and in which He would fain make His abode forever, driven out from it by the laughter and jesting with which we were making its consecrated walls to resound. How can He dwell in a temple which, from being a house of God and a house of prayer, we have turned into a place of merchandise, a hall of revelry, a haunt of mirth and song?

I do not mean, as I have said before, that the saint is ever to be gloomy. No. Gloom and melancholy are not our portion. "The lines have fallen unto us in pleasant places." They are not the inmates of a soul that has tasted the joy of pardon and is walking in light, as a happy child with a loving father. But true joy is a serious thing. Its fountains are deep. It is the waking up of the heart's deep springs. Mirth and levity are not joy. They are too shallow to deserve the name.

Like the sun-flash on a stagnant pool, they are a mere surface gleam of light. There is nothing in them of the calm radiance illuminating the ocean depths many a fathom down, as if the waters themselves were a mass of solid sunshine, and remaining amid the heaving of the billows, unbroken and unobscured. In coming to Him, who is the fountain of all gladness, the saint of God bids farewell to gloom. Tribulation he may have—nay, must have—but not gloom. That has left him forever since the day he knew the Savior, and opened his ears to the joyful sound. Peace is now his heritage.

But still it is not levity that is his portion. It is joy. And this joy is not only far superior to this vain mirth, but it is utterly inconsistent with it. This levity is as much an enemy to real joy as it is to holiness and spirituality. Hence, it must be rooted up. God cannot suffer it in His children. His desire is that they should set their affections on things above. This element of earthliness must be purged out. They must be made solemn and thoughtful. To this end He visits them with chastisement. In a moment, perhaps, He smites them to the dust; or, by some slower but withering, crushing calamity, He slays and casts out that foolishness which had wrought itself into the very texture of their being.

His purpose is to make them thoughtful and solemn. He lays on them accordingly something that will make them think. The blow prostrates them, and in a moment all levity is put to flight. They cannot laugh and jest now when their home is desolate and their heart is bleeding. They are withdrawn from intercourse with an airy, shadowy world and sent into the very inmost recesses of their spiritual being, or forward to the infinite eternity, whose vastness they had been but little alive to.

Trials awaken us to a sense of our self-pleasing ways and our indifference to the condition of the world we live in, not only as being a world of sin, but thoroughly, and all over, a world of misery. They bring us into contact with solid certainties and that produces thoughtfulness. They make us "acquainted with grief" and that drives off all levity. Sorrow and levity keep no companionship. It is through tears that truth is best seen. When looked at through this medium, objects assume their right proportions and take their proper level. Shadows then evaporate. Realities compass us about, and these make us solemn. Shadows only make us light and vain. They never stir the depths of our being, but merely flit around its surface.

Thus God solemnizes His saints, and brings them in this respect into closer sympathy with the mind of Christ. All was solemnity with Him. There was no levity ever found in Him. Everything about Him was serene, yet everything was solemn. And the nearer we are brought to resemble Him, the more will this calm, happy solemnity possess us. We shall live not only wakeful but solemn lives. Our whole deportment will speak the depth of the serenity that dwells within. Our looks and tones with all be solemn, and will of themselves testify for God and condemn the world. We shall be men awake and alive, men zealous and in earnest; men who have no relish for levity, because it is incompatible with the deep peace which is their better portion, and who feel that they have no time for it, because eternity is so near.

Yes, a near eternity rebukes and banishes frivolity. Even apart from positive trial this is its tendency. It is the eternal lifetime that makes the lifetime of earth such a solemn thing. Sever the living here from the living hereafter, and man's longest time on earth is little more in importance than the flutter of a leaf, his death no more than the falling of a blossom. But fasten on the infinite and the eternal to our present existence, and everything in life becomes mighty, momentous, solemn. The briefest moment that comes and goes is the meeting place of two eternities. Traversing this narrow pass, with rocks on either side of infinite ascent and lost in impenetrable midnight, how can we fail to be solemnized unless our eyes be closed or our reason gone! The pang that shoots through our frame and makes each fiber quiver would be quite endurable were it but for a moment, were it to die and be buried with us in the same tomb, were there no capacity of eternal anguish in our nature, or no eternity in which that capacity must develop itself. The sting of a moment is a trifle, but the eternal stinging of the undying worm is terrific beyond all utterance. In like manner the thrill of fresh joy which makes the whole man throb with delight would scarce be worth the having or the losing were it only like the lightning, flashing out in its brightness and then quenched forever. But a nature gifted with faculties for infinite enjoyment, and with a whole eternity in which these joyous buds shall expand themselves, turns all our life into a deep and awful reality. A flower that folds up its leaves and withers down at sunset may be carelessly trodden underfoot; but a star that shall roll around forever in its orbit, either effulgent in beauty or dark in the gloom of its own chaos, is an object of wonder and awe.

Such is the life of man! Not the life of one man or some men, but of every man. By itself it may seem a plaything, a mere insect's life; but in connection with the everlasting future, it becomes awfully real and solemn in its aspect. We may be noble and famed upon the earth, or we may be poor, unlettered, hard-toiling men, still our life is a vast reality. It is no mere shadow, or rainbow, or vision of the night, but an unconceivable reality in all its parts, great or small.

Such especially is the life of the saint! He not only knows that there is an eternity, but he has seen and felt it. Each hour he is looking out upon it like a traveler looking over a dark and infinite precipice which flanks the road on which he is passing along. He not only knows that there is such a thing as forgiveness and eternal life, but he has found them, he has tasted them; his eyes have been opened, and he has now come

into the very midst of realities. They compass him about on
every side. And especially as he "looks for that blessed hope,
even the glorious appearing" of the Lord, he feels what a
solemn life he is called upon to lead, and levity and mirth
as ill become him as they would have done the High Priest,
when standing within the veil under the immediate vision of
the glory.

Even without the positive infliction of chastisement there
is enough to solemnize a saint in what he sees and knows
of things as they are. A dying world, a groaning creation,
a curse-laden earth, a divided, bleeding church, an absent
bridegroom—these are at all times enough to subdue and
soften a believer's frame. And thus he walks through earth
like Paul after he had been in the third heaven—an inhabitant
of another star—one who has his conversation in heaven—
who is too happy ever to be gloomy, but too happy also ever
to be light or vain.

12

The Warning

Affliction is full of warnings. It has many voices and these of the most various kinds. It speaks counsel, it speaks rebuke, it speaks affection. But it speaks warning too. Let us hear some of its words of warning.

1. *It says, "Love not the world, neither the things that are in the world. If any man love the world, the love of the Father is not in him (1 John 2:15).* There is no enforcement of this warning so solemn as that which affliction gives. It exposes the world's hollowness and says, "love not." It shows us what a withering gourd its beauty is and says, "love not." It points out to us its hastening doom and says, "love not." It declares the utter impossibility of loving both the world and the Father, "If any man love the world, the love of the Father is not in him." "Know ye not that the friendship of the world is enmity with God?" There can be no companionship between God and the world. They cannot dwell together under the same roof or in the same heart.

2. *It says, "Take heed and beware of covetousness" (Luke 12:15).* Riches cannot help, neither earthly comfort avail us in the hour of grief. They cannot dry up tears, nor reunite broken bonds. They cannot heal the living, nor bring back the dead. They profit not in the day of darkness. Their vanity and

emptiness cannot then be hidden. "Thou fool, this night thy soul shall be required of thee, then whose shall those things be which thou hast provided?" It is then we find that we need a "treasure in the heaven that faileth not." "I counsel thee to buy of me gold tried in the fire, that thou mayest be rich."

3. *It says, "abstain from all appearance of evil" (1 Thess. 5:22).* "Hate even the garments spotted by the flesh." It is not the flesh merely that we are to hate, but even its garments. Nor is it the garments dyed and defiled with the flesh, but even "spotted" with it. It is not merely abstain from evil, but from all appearance of evil. Suffering teaches us to shrink from sin—even from the remotest and most indirect connection with it. It says, "Oh, do not that abominable thing which I hate!"

4. *It says, "Grudge not one against another" (James 5:9).* Let there be no halfhearted affection in the family of God. Let there be no envy, no jealousy, no misunderstandings among the brethren. Why should we be less than friends who are both fellow-sufferers and fellow-soldiers here? Why should we, who are sharers in a common danger and a common exile, bear for each other aught but the sympathies of an intense affection? Why should we not love one another with a pure heart fervently? Yet oftentimes it needs affliction to teach us this, to remove our jealousies, and to draw us together as brethren in sympathy and love.

5. *It says, "Keep yourselves from idols" (1 John 5:21).* If there be one remaining idol, break it in pieces and spare it not. Nothing is so fruitful a cause of suffering as idolatry. Nothing so forcibly displays the vanity of our idols as suffering. It is with this whip of cords that Christ scourges out of us the buyers and sellers—suffering no earthly traffic to proceed in His Father's house.

I give these warnings merely as specimens, a few out of many which might be adduced. There is no room for citing more, though more might easily be found. The two great points against which the warnings of chastisement are directed seem to be selfishness and worldliness. To scourge these thoroughly out of us is God's design.

1. *Selfishness.* "All seek their own, not the things that are Jesus Christ's." This was Paul's complaint, not of the ungodly, but of the churches of Christ. It was the selfishness he saw in the saints that gave occasion to these sorrowful words.

This selfishness is of various kinds, and shows itself in various ways. It is selfishness in reference to the things of Christ; or in reference to the church of Christ; or in reference to the work given us to do; or in reference to the sacrifices we are called upon to undergo, and the toils we are called upon to endure. It would be easy to show how God's chastisements are pointed at all these forms of selfishness, aiming deadly blows at each one of them from the outermost to the innermost circle. But this is too large a field. We shall merely take up the first, and even it we can only touch upon. It is the most important of them all, and stands so connected with the rest that whatever uproots it destroys the other also.

Selfishness, in reference to the things of Christ, obviously springs from coldness towards Christ Himself. A preference of self to Christ is its root and source. Anything, therefore, that tends to obscure or keep out of view the person of Christ must lead to selfishness. It may be the love of the world; it may be the love of the creature, it may be the love of man's applause. There are the dark bodies that eclipse the glory of a living Savior and nourish self. But these are not all. Satan has deeper devices still. He brings in religion between us and the Savior! Religious acts, ordinances, duties, are all turned by him into so many instruments for exalting self and lowering the Savior. But even this is not all. He has a subtler device

still for these last days. He is trying to make the work of
Christ a substitute for His person, to fix attention so much
upon the one as to exclude the other. The result of this is
a thoroughly selfish and sectarian religion. I know this is
delicate ground, but the evil is an augmenting one and ought
to be made known.

There are not a few who are so occupied with truth that
they forget "the true one," so occupied with faith that they
lose sight of its personal object, so given to dwelling upon
the work of Christ that they overlook His person. They seem
to regard the latter subject as a matter, if not beyond them,
at least one about which it will be time enough to concern
themselves when they see Him face to face. What He is seems
a question of small importance, provided they know that He
has accomplished a work by which they may secure eternal
life. "We are forgiven," they say, "we have peace—all is
well." They take but little interest in the person of Him who
has purchased these blessings. The redemption is all, and the
Redeemer is nothing, or, at least, very little! The sufficiency
of His work is all, the glory and excellence of His person,
nothing! What is this but selfishness? We get all the benefit
we can out of the work of Christ, and then leave Him alone!
And this selfishness introduces itself everywhere into the
actions and thinking of this class. We can trace it in the mold
of their doctrines. Their views of the atonement are selfish,
being framed not upon the principle of how God is to get His
purpose fulfilled and His glory displayed, but simply of how
a sinner is to be saved. Their views of Jehovah's sovereignty
and electing grace are selfish, being just so many devices for
taking the sinner out of God's hands and placing him in His
own. Their views of the Spirit's work are selfish, being just an
attempt to make His aid appear less absolutely indispensable
and man's own skill and strength of very considerable avail
in the matter of salvation. But even where those selfish views
of doctrine have not been adopted, there is a latent tendency

toward selfishness among many, which can only be ascribed to their neglect of the person of Christ.

But what has chastisement to do with this? Much every way. Chiefly in this that it throws us more entirely for consolation and strength upon the person of the Savior. Never do we feel more brought into contact with a living personal Savior than in our days of sorrow. It is Jesus— Jesus alone—Jesus Himself—whom we feel to be absolutely necessary. The truth is precious; His work is precious; but it is with Him that we have chiefly to do; it is to Him that we pour out our sorrows.

Thus by creating a necessity for our leaning on the person of Jesus (blessed necessity!) affliction strikes at that which was the root of selfishness. By bringing before us another and far more glorious self, it absorbs our own miserable self, till in the person of Jesus we lose sight of our own selves altogether. There is nothing that so makes us acquainted with Christ Himself as sorrow; and hence, there is nothing so efficacious in eradicating self. It is God's cure for selfishness. It is His way of making us seek, not our own, but the things that are Jesus Christ's. It is His way of carrying us beyond truth even to "him that is true." Truth is precious, but in itself it is cold. But the glory of the gospel is this, that it carries us up beyond truth to its living fountainhead. Nay, it brings us into the very bosom of Him who came out of the Father's bosom and has now returned to it, carrying with Him all those whom the Father hath given Him, there with Him to abide in happy fellowship, world without end.

This, however, is a large subject, and these are but a few hints. We cannot, however, pursue them further here. We pass on to notice the other evil against which the rebukes of God are directed.

2. *Worldliness.* We have seen that God's cure for selfishness is the setting before us of another self to absorb our own in

the person of Jesus. We have now to see that His cure for worldliness is the bringing before us of another world, more glorious than that which He calls on us to forsake. There is no thorough cure for it but this. It is want of faith that makes us worldlings; and when the believing eye gets fixed on the world to come, then we learn to set our affections on things above. So long, however, as all here is bright, we are content with them; we allow ourselves to sink down and settle quietly among the things of earth. But when God unroofs our dwelling, or tears up its foundation by an earthquake, then we are forced to look upward and seek a better and more enduring portion. Many such shocks, however, are often needed before our souls are broken off from their cleaving to the dust.

The opposite of worldliness is heavenly mindedness or spiritual mindedness. This, the new relish which the Holy Spirit imparts at conversion, in some measure produces. But it is feeble. It easily gives way. It is not keen enough to withstand much temptation. God's wish is to impart a keener relish for the things of God and to destroy the relish for the things of time. This He effects by blighting all objects in which there was earthly sweetness, so that by being deprived of objects to "mind" on earth, it may of necessity be led to "mind" the things above. He dries up all the "nether springs" of earthly joy, that we may betake ourselves to the "upper springs" which can never fail.

There is much worldliness among the saints. There is worldliness in their motives and actions, worldliness in their domestic life and in their intercourse with society, there is worldliness in the arrangements of their households and in the education of their families; there is worldliness in their expenditure, so much being laid out for self, so little for God; there is worldliness in their religious schemes, and movements, and societies; there is worldliness in their reading, and in their conversation; there is, in short, too much of the spirit of earnest worldliness about their whole deportment, and little of calm, happy superiority to the things of earth. They are fretted, disturbed, bustled just like the world. They grudge labor, or fatigue, or expense, or annoyance in the cause of Christ, or in serving their fellow men. They have much of earth, little of heaven about them. They are not large-hearted, openhanded—willing to spend and be spent, unmoved and unruffled, as those whose eye is ever set on the incorruptible inheritance on which they so soon shall enter. They are low and unaspiring in the things of God.

Perhaps there are few things against which we require to be more warned than against this spirit of worldliness. The church is very prone to forget her pilgrim character in this present evil world and to live as a citizen of earth. Her dignity as the eternally chosen of the Father is lost sight of; her hope as the inheritor of the glory and the kingdom of the Son is obscured. And oh, how much of sorrow she is preparing for herself by thus losing sight of her calling! What desolation may be even now hovering over the tabernacle of many a saint, because they will not come out and be separate, because they refuse to be "strangers on the earth as all their fathers were." Sad it is, indeed, that we should need affliction to teach us this!

Why should we whose home and treasure are above, ever again seek our home or our treasure here? Why should we stoop from our heavenly elevation to mingle again with the company which we have forsaken? Have we repented of our choice? Are we ashamed of our pilgrim staff and our pilgrim weeds? Surely not. Oh, if to be a stranger on earth is to be divided from sin and sinful appetites, from the seducing vanities and worthless mockeries of the world, from the fascinating beauty and perilous splendor of this decaying scene—if to be a stranger on earth is to be a friend of God, a member of the heavenly household, an expectant of the kingdom, an heir apparent of the crown of glory—who would not be a stranger here?

What higher honor would we seek than to share the homelessness of Jesus, the homelessness of the church from the beginning? Why should we seek to enter into nearer fellowship and dearer relationship with such a world as this? If we knew of no fairer heritage, we might not be wondered at for lusting after our forsaken pleasures. But we have the pleasures that are at God's right hand forever, and what are earth's allurements to us? What to us are the sights and sounds of earth, who "shall see the king in his beauty," and hear His voice, into whose lips grace is poured? What to us is the green fertility of earth, who shall enter into the possession of the new earth, when "the winter is past, the rain over and gone"? What to us is the gay glory of a city's wealth and pomp, who shall be made citizens of the New Jerusalem, where dwells the glory of God and of the Lamb, whose foundations are of precious stones, whose walls are of jasper, whose gates are of pearl, whose streets and pavements are of transparent gold? Let us, then, "pass the time of our sojourning here in fear." Let our loins be girt about and our lamps burning, and let us be as men ready to go forth to meet our returning Lord. If we watch not, if we reject the warning, our chastisement will be sharp and sore. The present seems a time of peculiar warning to the saints. Many are lying under the rebukes of the Lord. Judgment has begun at the house of God. God is dealing very closely and very solemnly with His own. On many a saint at this moment is His rod lying heavily, for He would fain warn and arouse them ere the evil day arrive. He is dealing with them as He dealt with Lot on the night before the desolation of Sodom. Let the saints, then, be warned. Let them be zealous and repent and do their first works. Come out, be separate, touch not the unclean thing! Put off the works of darkness; put on the armor of light. He is calling on them to get up to a higher level in the spiritual life, to have done with wavering, indecision, and compromise. He is calling on them to consider the apostle and High Priest of their profession and walk in His steps. He is calling on them to look at the cloud of witnesses, and lay aside every weight, especially that sin (of unbelief) which doth so easily beset them, and to run with patience the race set before them— "looking unto Jesus."

Church of the living God, be warned! Please not thyself, even as Jesus pleased not Himself. Live for Him, not for thyself; for Him, not for the world. Walk worthy of thy name and calling, worthy of Him who bought thee as His bride, worthy of thine everlasting inheritance.

Up, too, and warn the world! The chastisements that are falling so thickly on thee are forerunners of the fiery shower that is preparing for the earth. Up, then, and warn them— urge and entreat them to flee from gathering wrath. They have no time to lose, neither hast thou. The last storm is on the wing. Its dark skirts are already visible in the heavens. Judgment has begun at the house of God, and if so, what shall the end be of them that obey not the gospel of God!

13

The Recollections

"He hath made his wonderful works to be remembered" (Ps. 111:4). Yes, they are for "everlasting remembrance." They are not meant to be forgotten, and therefore, they are so made as to render forgetfulness almost impossible. Still we lose sight of them. They pass away "like a tale that is told."

Among the most wonderful of God's works are His chastisements. They are to be specially remembered by us. In themselves they are worthy of this. In their connection with us more so. None are so ineffaceable, for none are written so deep upon the heart. They are entwined with all that we feared or hoped in other days. They are "graven with an iron pen, and with lead in the rock for ever." No pen is like that of sorrow for writing indelibly upon the soul. Simply, as sorrow, God's dealings with us are not likely to be soon forgotten. We take pleasure in recalling our tears and griefs. But this is often mere selfish melancholy, brooding in solitude over a strange history. Sometimes, too, it is pride. We take proud pleasure in thinking that none has ever suffered as we have done.

Sometimes it is worldly sentiment, sitting down to muse over faded blossoms, or to recall the images of suns long set, or it may be to contrast the decay of earth with the abiding beauty of yon unwrinkled azure.

But this is not what God desires. It is not merely the remembrance of sorrow that He seeks, but of sorrow as

chastisement—of sorrow as linked all along with His gracious dealings toward us. The natural heart separates these
two things. It remembers the one but forgets the other
and so frustrates God's design. Himself He ever presents
to us; Himself He strives to keep before us, not simply as
connected with all our present and all our future history, but
as inseparably entwined with all the past.

It was thus that He expressed His mind to Israel regarding
this very thing. "Thou shalt remember all the way which the
Lord thy God led thee these forty years in the wilderness, to
humble thee, and to prove thee, to know what was in thine
heart, whether thou wouldest keep his commandments, or
no. And he humbled thee, and suffered thee to hunger, and
fed thee with manna, which thou knewest not, neither did thy
fathers know; that he might make thee know that man doth
not live by bread only, but by every word that proceedeth
out of the mouth of the Lord doth man live. Thy raiment
waxed not old upon thee, neither did thy foot swell these
forty years. Thou shalt also consider in thine heart, that, as
a man chasteneth his son, so the Lord thy God chasteneth
thee" (Deut. 8:2–5).

These recollections of the wilderness He wished to write
upon Israel's heart forever. He evidently lays much stress on
this. He would not have them lose the benefit of their desert
wanderings, and His desert dealings. They were too precious
to be forgotten. Forty years close and solitary intercourse with
God in such various ways ought to have taught them much,
both of Him and of themselves, which deserved everlasting
memory. Each name had some wondrous scene attached to
it; each rock had its story to tell. Their enemies and dangers,
their hunger and their thirst, the manna and the water, the
murmurings and the thanksgiving, their journeys and their
encampments, their raiment that waxed not old, their shoes
that were as iron and brass, their feet that swelled not, and
above all, the cloud that rested over them, and the tent of

Jehovah that was pitched in the midst of them—these were memorable scenes. And they were all connected with the wilderness. Never before had there been such an assemblage of wondrous dealings, and never since has anything like this been seen on earth. It could occur but once. And that once was to furnish matter for remembrance to Israel, descending as a precious heritage to their children and to their children's children forever.

It is thus with the saint in reference to his desert days and desert trials. They must not be forgotten as if they had served their purpose. They must be ever rising before us—not merely preserved in memory like the manna in the ark, but brought forth to feed upon every day. In this way sorrow may be most profitable to us long after its bitterness has passed away. It may furnish us with a treasury of blessings for a lifetime. It may be a mine of gold to us all our days. We are too little aware of this. We look on trial too much as we do upon a passing shower, which falls and then is gone. Whereas, it is truly the smiting of the rock and the issuing forth of a new stream, whose waters are to keep us company through all our days of wandering. The benefits of chastisement should never be exhausted. They should be coming forth in freshness with every hour. Even when sitting calmly in the sunshine we may be drawing profit from the stormy past. This is consolation to the chastened soul; for how often in this way will a short sorrow be turned into lasting gladness. And it does seem as if what is thus obtained by us were a richer kind of blessing, a holier, deeper joy. Oh, let us remember past trials and carefully treasure them up as the choicest of our earthly possessions! The saint who has many of these to look back upon has some reason to glory in his inheritance.[1]

---

1. "Truly no cross should be old to us. We should not forget them, because years are come betwixt us and them, and cast them by hand as we do old clothes. We may make a cross old in time new in use, and as fruitful as in the beginning of it." —Samuel Rutherford

It is this that especially exercises that softening, mellowing influence which has been often observed in affliction. During the actual pressure of the sorrow there was less of this. Perhaps we were so stunned and stupefied as almost to be deprived of feeling. Or if we did feel, still there was so much of sharpness and bitterness about it that we were bruised rather than softened. There was such a struggle and such confusion of spirit that we sometimes wondered if we were profiting at all, and thought that the sorrow was too great to be productive of benefit.

But in the retrospect all is different. "No chastening for the present seemeth to be joyous but grievous; nevertheless, afterwards it yieldeth the peaceable fruits of righteousness unto them which are exercised thereby." The wound has ceased to bleed, and, though it will remain a scar forever, it is no longer open. It is then that the mellowing process goes on, and each remembrance of the past helps it forward. This is less perceptible than the others we are not so directly conscious of it; but its silent influence upon our character, our temper, our will, our judgment, is wonderful. The deathbed, the farewell, the funeral scene, the open tomb, the earth striking rudely on the coffin, the grave filled up, the turf rolled on by stranger hands—these are like swords going through the very vitals. But they sadden more than they soften. It is the remembrance of these scenes, the frequent visit to the closed tomb, the calm after inquiry into, and meditation upon, God's meaning in all this—it is these that so gently exercise a whole lifetime's influence upon the soul. They surround us with a softening atmosphere, and the light they shed down on us is the light of sunset, mellowed and shaded in its passage through the clouds of evening.

In another way also these recollections are precious. They teach us that God is true. The trials themselves taught us this; but their remembrance teaches us this more. And it is a lesson which even the saints need much to learn. Even they need to be taught how surely He is the Amen, "the faithful and the true," and in all that He has spoken to His church He has spoken truly. What refreshing confirmations of this do we gather as we call to mind the past and see how the Lord hath led us! We can add our Amen every day to what Joshua declared to Israel on his deathbed. "Behold, this day I am going the way of all the earth: and ye know in all your hearts and in all your souls, that not one thing hath failed of all the good things which the Lord your God spake concerning you; all are come to pass unto you, and not one thing hath failed thereof" (Josh. 23:14).

Yes, "all things work together for good"—the past as well as the present. And thus the stream of which we drink is a swelling one. Innumerable tributaries are flowing into it. This year it is "to the ankles." Next year it will be "to the knees." After that it will rise "to the loins." And as it reaches the ocean, bearing us calmly on its bosom, it will be a great river "that cannot be passed over." Yet, oh, how little have the saints learned to prize these memorials of chastisement, these recollections of the wilderness, which are so rich in instruction, so fraught with blessing and with joy!

14

The Consolation

To bring many sons unto glory, was the end for which the Son of God took flesh and died. This was no common, no inferior object. So vast and worthy did Jehovah deem it that it pleased Him for the attaining of it to "make the captain of their salvation perfect through sufferings" (Heb. 2:10). It was an object worthy of the God "for whom are all things, and by whom are all things." It was an object glorious enough to render it "becoming" in Him to make Jesus pass through suffering and death, and to justify the Father in not sparing His only begotten Son.

They for whom God has done all this must be very precious in His sight. He must be much in earnest indeed to bless them and to take them to be with Him forever. As He so delighted in Enoch that He could no longer bear the separation and the distance, but took him to be with Him without tasting death, and long ere he had run the common race of man, so with His saints. He is making haste to bring them to glory, for the day of absence has been long.

The glory which He has in reserve for them must be surpassing glory, for it was to bring them to it that He was willing to bruise His Son and to put Him to grief. Eye hath not seen it; ear hath not heard it; it is far beyond what we can comprehend, yet it is all reality. God is not ashamed to be called our God because He hath prepared for us a city. Were that city not worthy of Himself He would be ashamed to have called Himself by the name of "our God." For that implies large blessings on His part, and it leads to large expectations on ours, expectations which He cannot disappoint. He did not count this glory to be bought for us at too dear a rate, even though the price was the sufferings of His only begotten Son. If, then, God thus estimated the glory to which we were to be brought, shall not we do the same? If He thought it worth all the sufferings of His Son, shall we not think it worth our poor sufferings here? Shall we not say, "I reckon that the sufferings of this present time are not worthy to be compared with the glory which shall be revealed in us" (Rom. 8:18)?

This is consolation. It is that which most naturally occurs to us, and it is both scriptural and effectual. This is what is usually presented to the afflicted saint, and it is what he feels to be very precious and suitable. But though the most common and the most natural consolation, it is by no means the only one. Let us suggest a few others.

1. *Jesus weeps with us.* "In all our affliction he is afflicted." He knows our sorrows, for He has passed through them all, and therefore He feels for us. He is touched with the feeling of our griefs as well as of our infirmities. Man—very man—man all over, even in His glory He enters most fully into the fellowship of our burdens and sorrow, whatever these may be, for there is not one which He did not taste when He "dwelt among us" here. His is sympathy, deep, real, and true. It is no fiction, no fancy. We do not see His tears falling upon us; neither do we clasp His hand nor feel the beating of His heart against ours.

But still His communion with us in suffering is a reality. We may not understand how it can be. But He understands it; and He can make us feel it, whether we can comprehend it or not.

2. *We are made partakers of Christ's sufferings.* What honor is this! We are baptized with His baptism; we drink of His cup, we are made like Him in sorrow as we shall hereafter be made like Him in joy! How soothing and sustaining! If reproach, and shame, and poverty are ours, let us remember that they were His also. If we have to go down to Gethsemane, or up to the cross, let us think that He was there before us. It is when keeping our eye on this that we are brought somewhat to realize the feeling of the apostle when he "rejoiced in his sufferings" for the church, as filling "up that which is behind [literally the leavings of Christ's sufferings] of the afflictions of Christ in my flesh for his body's sake, which is the church" (Col. 1:24). To be treated better than Christ was is neither what a thoughtful soul could expect, nor what a loving heart could desire.

3. *Suffering is the family lot.* This we have already dwelt upon, and we recur to it simply to present it more prominently as a consolation. The path of sorrow is no unfrequented way. All the saints have trodden it. We can trace their footprints there. It is comforting, nay, it is cheering to keep this in mind. Were we cast fettered into some low dungeon, would it not be a consolation to know that many a martyr had been there before us, would it not be cheering to read their names written with their own hands all round the ancient walls? Such is the solace we may extract from all suffering, for the furnace into which we are cast has been consecrated by many a saint already.

4. *All things work together for our good.* Nothing is unsuitable, unseasonable, or unprofitable. Out of all evil comes good to the saints; out of all darkness comes light; out of all sorrow comes joy. Each pang, sharp or slight, is doing its work—the very work which God designs, the very work which we could not do without. The bed of sorrow is not only like Solomon's

chariot, all "paved with love," but, like it, it moves on with mighty swiftness, bearing us most blessedly onward to the inheritance of the undefiled. The forces of earth, unless they all bear in one line, or nearly so, tend to counteract each other and arrest the common impulse. But the forces which God brings to bear upon us in affliction are all directly and necessarily impulsive. Come from what quarter they may, or from opposite quarters all at once, they still bear us successfully forward. "All things work together for good." "All things are ours."

5. *There is special grace for every trial.* As trials bring to light the weakness that is in us, so they draw out to meet the strength of God—new resources of strength and grace which we never knew before. In affliction we may be quite sure of learning something more of God than we were acquainted with before, for it is just in order to furnish an opportunity for bringing out this and showing it to us that He sends the trial. How little should we know of Him were it not for sorrow! What fullness of blessing comes out to us, what riches of love are spread out before us in the dark and cloudy day!

6. *Affliction is our fullest opportunity for glorifying God.* It is on earth that He expects to get glory from us, glory such as angels cannot give, glory such as we shall not be able to give hereafter. It is here that we are to preach to angels; it is here we are to show to them what a glorious God is ours. Our whole life below is given us for this. But it is especially in sorrow and under infirmity that God looks for glory from us. What a God-honoring thing to see a struggling, sorrowing child of earth cleave fast to God, calmly trusting in Him, happy and at rest in the midst of storm and of suffering! What a spectacle for the hosts of heaven! Now, then, is the time for the saints to give glory to the Lord their God. Let them prize affliction as the very time and opportunity for

doing so most of all. Let them use such a season well. And oh, what consolation to think that affliction is really such a season! Ah, surely it is one which an angel might covet, which an archangel would gladly stoop to were that possible! They can glorify God much in heaven amid its glory and blessedness, but oh, not half so much as we can on earth amid suffering and shame!

7. *We are getting rid of sin.* Each pain is a nail driven through some sin, another blow inflicted on the flesh, destroying the very power of sinning. As we entered on our first life, sin fastened its chain upon us, and link after link twined itself about us. When we commenced our second and better life, these began one by one to untwine themselves. Affliction untwined them faster; and though it is not till we are laid on a deathbed or till Jesus comes that the last link of earth is thoroughly untwined or broken, still it is consolation to think that each successive trial is helping on the blessed consummation. A lifetime's sufferings would not be too long or too heavy, if by means of them we got rid of sin and sinful ways and tempers, and became more holy, more heavenly, more conformable to the image of the Lord. When first we believed in Jesus, we were "delivered from a present evil world." Yet this deliverance is not complete. The world and we have not yet fully parted company with each other. And, therefore, God drives affliction like a wedge between us and the world; or He sends it like a plowshare right across our most cherished hopes and brightest prospects till He thoroughly wearies us of all below. "He hath made me weary," said Job. Nor do we wonder at the complaint. Wearisome nights were his. The "ploughers ploughed upon his back," and drew many a long furrow there. He might well be weary. So with us. God makes us weary, too, weary all over—thoroughly weary. We are weary of a present evil world, weary of self, weary of sin, weary of suffering, weary of this mortal body,

weary of these vile hearts, weary of earth—weary of all but
Jesus! Of Him no trial can weary us. Suffering only endears
Him the more. Blessed suffering—that makes Him appear
more precious and the world viler; that brings Him nearer to
our hearts and thrusts the world away!

8. *We are preparing for usefulness while here.* We have but a few
years below, and it concerns us much that these should be
useful years. We have but one life, and it must be laid out
for God. But we need preparation for usefulness. We need a
thorough breaking down, a thorough emptying, a thorough
bruising. God cannot trust us with success till we are thus
laid low. We are not fit to receive it; nor would He get the
glory. Therefore He sends sore and heavy trials in order to
make us vessels fit for the Master's use. And oftentimes we
see that the heaviest trials are forerunners of our greatest
usefulness. When we are entirely prostrated and crushed,
then it is safe to grant us success, for God gets all the glory.
And oh, what wonders has God often done by bruised reeds!
Yea, it is the bruised reed that is oftenest the instrument in
His hand for working His mighty signs and wonders. What
consolation is this! Suffering is stripped of half its bitterness
if it thus brings with it a double portion of the Spirit, and fits
for double usefulness on earth.

9. *We have the Holy Spirit as our Comforter.* He is mighty to
comfort as well as to sanctify. His name is "the Comforter."
His office is to console. And in the discharge of this office
He puts forth His power, not only mediately and indirectly
through the Word, but immediately and directly upon the
soul, sustaining and strengthening it when fainting and
troubled. It is consolation unspeakable to know that there is a
hand, a divine and omnipotent hand, laid upon our wounded
spirit, not only upholding it, but drying up, as it were, the
very springs of grief within. In the day of oppressive sorrow,

when bowed down to the dust, what is it that we feel so much our need of as a hand that can come into close and direct contact with our souls to lift them up and strengthen them? For it is here that human consolation fails. Friends can say much to soothe us, but they cannot lay their finger upon the hidden seat of sorrow. They can put their arm around the fainting body, but not around the fainting spirit. To that they have only distant and indirect access. But here the heavenly aid comes in. The Spirit throws around us the everlasting arms, and we are invincibly upheld. We cannot sink, for He sustains, He comforts, He cheers. And who knows so well as He how to sustain, and comfort, and cheer?

10. *The time is short.* We have not a pilgrimage like Seth's or Noah's, or even like Abraham's to pass through. Ours is but a hand-breadth in comparison with theirs. We have not many days to suffer, nor many nights to watch, even though our whole life were filled with weary days and sleepless nights. "Our light affliction is but for a moment." And besides the briefness of our earthly span, we know that the coming of the Lord draweth nigh. This is consolation, for it tells not only of the end of our tribulation, but of the beginning of our triumph; nay, and not only of our individual rest from trouble; but of the rest and deliverance of the whole church together. For then the whole "body of Christ," waking or sleeping, shall be glorified with their glorified Lord, and everlasting joy shall be upon their heads. In the day of bereavement, the day of mourning over those who have fallen asleep in Jesus, this consolation is especially precious. Them that sleep in Jesus will God bring with Him. And if the Lord be near, the time of reunion may not be far off. They that lie down at evening have a whole night's slumber before them; but they who lie down toward morning have, it may be, but an hour or less till the dawn awakes them. So with the dead in Christ in these last days. They will not have long to sleep,

for it is now the fourth watch of the night, and the day-star is preparing to arise. What consolation! How it soothes the pain of parting! How it cheers the wounded spirit! "Awake, and sing, ye that dwell in dust," is now our watchword every day. We take our stand upon our watchtower, and look out amidst the darkness of night for the first streaks of morn. We lay our ear to the ground and listen that, amid all the discord of earth, the uproar of war, the tumults of the nations, we may catch the first sound of our Lord's chariot wheels— those chariot wheels that are to sweep in vengeance over the field of Armageddon, crushing the confederate nations leagued against the Lord and His Anointed, and also to bring to the bosom of the long-betrothed Bride, the Husband of her youth, the desire of her soul, for whom, amid tears and loneliness, she has waited for many a generation, many a century, in vain.

11. *All is love.* Affliction is the expression of paternal love. It is from the deepest recess of the fountain of love that sorrow flows down to us. And love cannot wrong us. It blesses, but cannot curse. Its utterances and actions are all of peace and gladness. It wants a larger vessel into which to empty itself, and a deeper channel through which to flow. That is all. It seeks to make us more susceptible of kindness, and then to pour that kindness in. Yes, love is the true, the one origin of the sharpest stroke that ever fell upon a bleeding heart. The truth is, there is no other way of accounting for affliction but this. Anger will not account for it, forgetfulness will not account for it, chance will not account for it. No, it is simply impossible to trace it to any cause but love. Admit this as its spring, and all is harmonious, comely, perfect. Deny it, and all is confusion, cruelty, and darkness. Chastising love is the faithfulest, purest, truest, tenderest, deepest of all. Let this be our consolation.

Beloved, "it is well." It is good to be afflicted. Our days

of suffering here we call days of darkness; hereafter they will seem our brightest and fairest. In eternity we shall praise Jehovah most of all for our sorrows and tears. So blessed shall they then seem to us that we shall wonder how we could ever weep and sigh. We shall then know how utterly unworthy we were of all this grace. We did not deserve anything, but least of all to be afflicted. Our joys were all of grace—pure grace—much more our sorrows. It is out of the "exceeding riches of the grace of God" that trial comes.

15

The Eternal Results

If we suffer we shall also reign with Him. Of this we are assured. Oneness in suffering here is the pledge of oneness in glory hereafter. The two things are inseparable. His shame is ours on earth; His glory shall be ours in heaven. Therefore, let us "rejoice, inasmuch as ye are partakers of Christ's sufferings; that, when his glory shall be revealed, ye may be glad also with exceeding joy" (1 Peter 4:13).

Truly the sufferings of this present life are not worthy to be compared with the glory which shall be revealed in us. The incorruptible crown is so surpassingly bright, and the "inheritance of the saints in light" so excellent that we may well be ashamed even to speak of present sorrow. How will the eternal light absorb the darkness here! How will the blessedness of the kingdom swallow up our earthly calamities and complaints! One hour of eternity, one moment with the Lord will make us utterly forget a lifetime of desolations. But more than this, our troubles now do but enhance the coming joy. Our affliction is not only "light," not only "but for a moment," but it worketh for us a far more exceeding and eternal weight of glory. Our sorrows here are but adding to the weight of our eternal crown. In what way they do so we are not told. It is sufficient that we know upon God's authority that such is really the case. Need we then grudge or rebel against that which is preparing for us such glad and sure results? As to the nature of the recompense, God has revealed much to us, at least insofar as human language and earthly figures can set it forth. In the epistles to the seven churches of Asia we have the fullest opening of this manifold reward. For "him that overcometh," there is an abundant "weight of glory" provided. To each of the seven conquerors there is a separate reward, and taking them all together, what a fullness of infinite blessing is comprised in this sevenfold recompense! To one conqueror there is promised the "tree of life." To another, the "crown of life" and deliverance from the second death. To another, "the hidden manna," the "white stone," and in it the new, the unknown name. To another, power over the nations, the iron rod of rule, the morning-star. To another, the white raiment and enrollment in the book of life. To another, the honor of being made a pillar in the temple of God, and of having written on him the name of God and the name of His city—God's own new name. To another, a seat upon the throne of Christ, joint dominion with Him in His kingdom, joint heirship with Him in His inheritance, for "he that overcometh shall inherit all things." True, this recompense is only "to him that overcometh." It is a lifetime battle—a wrestling not only with flesh and blood, but with principalities and powers, with the rulers of the darkness of this world, with spiritual wickedness in high places. But then, however desperate the warfare, it is not forever. Nay, it is brief, very brief. Its end is near, very near. And with the end come triumph, and honor, and songs of victory. Then, too, there follows peace, and the return of the war-worn soldier to his quiet dwelling.

> *Now the soft peace-march beats,*
> *home, brothers, home.*

This is the joy of the saint. He has fought a good fight, he has finished the course, he has kept the faith. Henceforth there is laid up for him the crown of righteousness. His battle is over, and then for him there are rest and home. Home!

Yes, home. And what a home for us to return to and abide in forever! A home prepared before the foundation of the world, a home in the many mansions, a home in the innermost circle of creation, nearest the throne and heart of God, a home whose peace shall never be broken by the sound of war or tempest, whose brightness shall never be overcast by the remotest shadow of a cloud. How solacing to the weary spirit to think of a resting-place so near, and that resting-place our Father's house where we shall hunger no more, neither thirst any more, where the sun shall not light on us, nor any heat, where the Lamb that is in the midst of the throne shall feed us and lead us to living fountains of waters, and God shall wipe away all tears from our eyes.

The time is at hand. The church's conflicts are almost over. Its struggles and sorrows are nearly done. A few more years, and we shall either be laid quietly to rest, or caught up into the clouds to meet our coming Lord. A few more broken bonds, and then we shall be knit together in eternal brotherhood with all the scattered members of the family. A few more suns shall rise and set, and then shall ascend in its strength the one upsetting sun. A few more days shall dawn and darken, and then shall shine forth the one unending day. A few more clouds shall gather over us, and then the firmament shall be cleared forever. A few more sabbaths shall come around, filling the sum of our privileges and completing our allotment of time, and then the everlasting sabbath shall begin. But a few brief years, and we shall "enter in through the gates into the city," sitting down beneath the shadow of the tree of life, feeding upon the hidden manna, and drinking of the pure river clear as crystal, which proceedeth out of the throne of God and of the Lamb. But a few years and we shall see His face, and His name shall be upon our foreheads.

These are some of the eternal results, results which are mightily heightened and enhanced by our tribulations here. For affliction not only profits us much just now, but it will serve us much in eternity. Then we shall discover how much we owe to it. All that it is doing for us, we know not now, but we shall know hereafter. It is preparing for us a "more abundant entrance," a weightier crown, a whiter robe, a sweeter rest, a home made doubly precious by a long exile and many sufferings here below.

Of these results we have only the foretaste now. The full brightness is in reserve, and we know that all that is possible or conceivable of what is good and fair and blessed shall one day be real and visible. Out of all evil there comes the good; out of sin comes holiness; out of darkness, light; out of death, life eternal; out of weakness, strength; out of the fading the blooming; out of a quenched planet, a sun for the universe; out of rottenness and ruin, comeliness and majesty; out of the curse, the blessing; and Resurrection shall prove the wondrous truth that it is the grave—the place of bones and dust—that is the womb of the incorruptible, the immortal, the glorious, the undefiled.

Our present portion, however, is but the earnest, not the inheritance. That is reserved for the appearing of the Lord. Here we see but through a glass darkly. It doth not yet appear what we shall be. We are but as wayfaring men, wandering in the lonely night, who see dimly upon the distant mountain peak the reflection of a sun that never rises here, but which shall never set in the "new heavens" hereafter. And this is enough. It comforts and cheers us on our dark and rugged way. It would not be enough hereafter, but it is enough just now. The wilderness will do for us till we cross into Canaan. The tent will do till the "city of habitation" comes. The joy of believing is enough till we enter on the joy of seeing. We are content with the "mountain of myrrh, and the hill of frankincense," until "the day break and the shadows flee away."

The Morning of Joy

Being
A Sequel to *The Night of Weeping*

"Joy cometh in the morning."
— Psalm 30:5

Preface

I have been asked, once and again, to follow up *The Night of Weeping* with *The Morning of Joy*, the words of David, in the 30th Psalm, having suggested the addition. After much thought and some hesitation I have done so.

The former work was meant to be complete in itself, presenting not merely the night-side of tribulation, but bringing out also, though less prominently, some of its day-hues. As, however, it has been thought incomplete, having in it so much more of *night* than of *day;* an endeavor has been made to complete it by drawing forward the eye to the scenes of morning, so soon to open upon us, in all their breadth and beauty. In this way we are led to forget the things that are behind, and to reach forward to those before, pressing towards the mark for the prize of our high calling. And the fuller, the truer, the more frequent our anticipations of promised glory are, the deeper and the richer will our consolations be.

Sitting down beneath the shadow of the cross, and reading in its inscription God's record of free love, our fears are put to flight and our souls find rest. Possessed of forgiveness and assured of the life that dies not, we feel that all is well with us. "Come life, come death," we can say, "come calm or storm, come gain or loss, come joy or grief, all is well." For "the work of righteousness is peace, and the effect of righteousness quietness and assurance for ever."

And surely this *is* much in the way of consolation, even though we had nothing more to cheer us. But it is not all. There is much more than this.

While sitting there God opens upon our eye a wide prospect, stretching far into eternity. Perhaps he sends trial, "breaking us with his tempest." Then he spreads out before us the vision of brightness for our comfort, and as the grief presses heavier, the vision enlarges on the view. The going down of our sun, though it covers earth with a shadow, draws the curtain from the firmament above us, and encircles us with the splendour of ten thousand stars. Then we not only are led to see that the greater portion of our being lies beyond either present joy or sorrow, but are also led to inquire into those outlying hopes, and to survey the whole breadth of that goodly inheritance, of which we are the heirs.

These inquiries and surveys are, as we shall see, most blessed in their nature, and purifying, as well as comforting, in their tendency. They are fraught with holiness and full of joy. They tend to make us forget the present in the future, and to assimilate us to the objects thus vividly presented to us. For, though it is true that "tears make the harvest of the heart to grow;" yet it is the anticipated light of the unrisen morning that *ripens* it.

This is more than mere *negative* consolation. It is positive and efficacious. The negative is, "Wherefore should a living man complain?" or, "There the wicked cease from troubling and the weary are at rest." This, so far as it goes, is precious. But God has given us something more than this. The hope which he furnishes is not merely the hope of a quiet close to this world's weariness, but the hope of infinite gladness which is then to begin. There is a passage in Job which exemplifies both of these very fitly. Groaning under the pressure of no common grief, he cries out,

> *Oh that thou wouldst hide me in the grave!*
> *That thou wouldst keep me secret!*
> *Till thy wrath be past.*

As if he would be glad to be hidden any where, even in the grave, from such calamities. But then this is not enough. This is mere *negative* comfort. It is the mere cessation of suffering.

And this does not content him. He bethinks himself, and cries out again,

> *Oh that thou wouldst appoint me a set time*
> *And remember me!*

He cannot bear the thought of always lying in the dust, even though it is a secure hiding-place from the storms of earth. He would not be forgotten there. He would have a time set, at the end of which God might remember him. Then abruptly he asks,

> *If a man die shall he live?*

and, evidently answering himself, "Yes, he shall live again," he calmly adds,

> *All the days of my appointed time will I wait,*
> *Till my* CHANGE *come.*

For it is resurrection-change he looks for, and rejoices in as his hope. When that day arrives the trumpet shall sound, the voice of God shall speak,—

> *Thou shalt call,*
> *And I will answer!*

But how is he so assured of being thus remembered of God? He knows how precious in his eyes is the dust of his saints,—

> *Thou wilt have a desire*
> *To the work of thine hands.*

Thus, though Job begins with what is merely negative, that is, the ending of his grief and shame, he cannot rest there, but presses on, in rapid hope, to the beginning of his joy and glory. It is the MORNING, with all its new life and reviving sunshine, that rises before his view, and from afar pours into him its healing light.

"The fashion of this world passeth away." This cheers

us, for it assures us that no grief shall live long. But the fashion of "the world to come" endures. This is unspeakably gladdening; for all that that better "age" brings with it shall abide for ever. The inheritance is vast, the city is "joyous," the mansions are many, the title is sure, and the possession is everlasting.

Jerusalem! Jerusalem!
Would God I were in thee!
Oh that my sorrows had an end,
Thy joys that I might see.

Thus sweetly sung one of Scotland's holiest sons in the olden time. Broken with many griefs, he thus poured out his soul,—weary and homesick, as a stranger here. And will not "night" fail in one of its objects, if it does not make us long for the "day"? Will not tribulation be frustrated if it do not stir within us this "earnest expectation," this "groaning within ourselves," this "fervent longing,"—this homesickness which the saints in other days felt so tenderly and truly? And all the more, because "now is our salvation nearer than when we believed;" for we have arrived at the last stage of our journey, and a few more days will suffice to bring us home.

Kelso, December 19, 1849.

1

The Anticipations

The church of God on earth is not what she seems; nay, is what she seems not. She is not a beggar, yet she seems one; she is a King's bride, yet she seems not. It was so with her Lord while here. He was not what men thought Him; He was what they thought Him not.

It is in this way that the world is put to shame, its thoughts confounded, its greatness abased before God. And it is in this way that divine wisdom gets large space over which to spread itself, step by step, and to open out its infinite resources slowly and with care, (like one exhibiting his treasures), that no part, no turn in all its windings may be left unobserved. It is not the result only that God desires that we should see and wonder at, but the process by which it is reached, so unlikely to effect it, yet so steadily moving forward to its end, and so strangely successful in bringing about that end. The planting of the "trees of God" in Eden, in full strength and fruitfulness at once, was not such an exhibition of wisdom as that which we ourselves see in yearly process before us, when God out of a small, shapeless seed brings a stately pine or palm.

In truth, this is the law of our world. It might not be so at first in Eden, when only the *result* was given to view; but it has been so since, and is so now, for God is showing us most minutely how "fearfully and wonderfully" all things

are made, and we among the rest, in soul and in body, in
our first birth and in our second, in our natural and in our
spiritual growth.

The tree, in winter, is not what it appears—dead; nay, it
is what it appears not—alive; full in every part, root, stem,
and branch, of vigorous though hidden vitality, a vitality
which frosts and storms are but maturing, not quenching.
All summer-life is there; all autumn fruitfulness is there;
though neither visible. It wraps up within itself the germs of
future verdure, and awaits the coming spring. So is it with
the church, in this age of wintry night; for it is both night
and winter with her. Her present condition ill accords with
her prospects. No one, in looking at her, could guess what
she either is or is to be; could conceive what God has in
store for her. For eye has nothing to do with the seeing of it,
nor ear with the hearing of it. No one, in observing her garb
or her deportment, or the treatment she meets with at the
hands of men, or the sharp, heavy discipline through which
she is passing, could take the measure of her hopes. Faith
finds difficulty in realizing her prospects, and she can hardly
at times credit the greatness of her heritage, when thinking
of what she is and remembering what she has been.

It often seems strange to us, and it must seem much more
so to unfallen beings, that saints should be found at all in such
a world—a world without God, a world of atheists—a world
that from the days of Cain has been the rejecter of His Son,
both as the sacrifice for sin and as the heir of all things. It
is not on such a spot that we should naturally expect to find
sons of God. Next to hell, it is the unlikeliest place for a soul
that loves God to dwell in, even for a day, and if a stranger,
traversing the universe in search of God's little flock, His
chosen ones, were to put to us the question, "Where are
they to be found?" certainly he would be astonished when
told that they were in that very world where Satan reigned,
and from which God had been cast out! Would he not

say, "Either this is a mistake and a chance, or else it is the very depth of unfathomable wisdom"? For we do not go to the crater's slope for verdure; nor for flowers to the desert; nor for the plants of heaven to the shores of the lake of fire. Yet it is so with the church. It is strange perhaps to find a Joseph in Egypt, or a Rahab in Jericho, or an Obadiah in the house of Ahab; but it is more amazing to find saints in the world at all.

Yet they are here. In spite of everything ungenial in soil and air, they are here. They never seem to become acclimatized, yet they do not die out, but are ever renewed. The enemy labors to uproot them, but they are ineradicable. Nay, they thrive and bear fruit. It is a miracle; but yet so it is. Here the great Husbandman is rearing His plants from generation to generation. Here the great Potter fashions His vessels. Here the great Master-builder hews and polishes the stones for His eternal temple.

Thus, then, one characteristic of the church is, the unlikeliness of her present to her future condition. It is this that marks her out, that isolates her, as a gem in the heart of a rock, as a vein of gold in a mine. Originally she belonged to the mass, but she was drawn apart from it, or it fell from off her and left her alone, like a pillar among ruins. Outwardly she retains much of her former self; but inwardly she has undergone a change that has assimilated her to "the world to come." Thus her affinities and her sympathies are all with that better world. Her dwelling is still here, and in external appearance she is much as she used to be; but the internal transformation has made her feel that this is not her home, and filled her with anticipations of the city and the kingdom to come, of which she has been made the heir. Her kindred according to the flesh are here, but she is now allied to Jehovah by the ties of blood, and this draws her soul upwards.

Cut off from a home and a heritage here, yet assured of

both hereafter, she of necessity lives a life of anticipation. Giving credit to the message of grace, and resting on the blood of Him through whose cross that grace came down to her, she anticipates her acquittal at the judgment. Realizing her oneness with the risen and ascended Christ, she feels as if already seated with Him in heavenly places. Looking forward to the arrival of the King, she anticipates the kingdom. In darkness she anticipates the light; in sorrow she anticipates the joy; in the night she anticipates the morning; in shame she anticipates the glory. "All are mine," she says "whether Paul, or Apollos, or Cephas, or the world, or life, or death, or things present, or things to come; all are mine; for I am Christ's, and Christ is God's." In these anticipations she lives. They make up a large portion of her daily being. They cheer her onward in spite of the rough wastes she has to pass through. They comfort her; or when they do not quite succeed in this, they at least calm and soothe her. They do not turn midnight into noon, but they make it less oppressive, and take off "the night side of nature."

"I am not what I seem," she says to herself, "and this is joy. I am not the beggared outcast that the world takes me for. I am richer far than they. They have their riches now, but mine are coming when theirs are gone. They have their joys now; but mine are coming when theirs have ended in eternal weeping. I live in the future; my treasure is in heaven, and my heart has gone up to be where my treasure is. I shall soon be seen to be what I now seem not. My kingdom is at hand; my sun is about to rise; I shall soon see the King in His beauty; I shall soon be keeping festival, and the joy of my promised morning will make me forget that I ever wept."

Thus she lives in the morning, ere the morning has come. She takes a wide sweep of vision, round and round, without a limit, for faith has no horizon; it looks beyond life, and earth, and the ages, into eternity.

Beyond the death-bed and beyond the grave, she sees

resurrection. Beyond the broken hearts and severed bands of time, she realizes and clasps the eternal love-links; beyond the troubles of the hour, and beyond the storm that is to wreck the world, she casts her eye, and feels as if transported into the kingdom that cannot be moved, as if already she had taken up her abode in the New Salem, the city of peace and righteousness. Beyond the region of the falling leaf she passes on to the green pastures, and sits down under the branches of the tree of life which is in the midst of the paradise of God. Losing sight of the bitterness of absence from the beloved of her heart, she enters the bridal-chamber and tastes the bridal joy; keeping festival even in the desert, and enjoying the sabbath rest amid the tumults of a stormy world.

2

The Night-Watch

We are not *of* the world, though we are in the world. So "we are not of the night"; though we are in the night. We are "children of the day;" we belong to the day, and the day belongs to us, as our true heritage, though it has not yet dawned. Hope rests there; and though deferred, will not always tarry, nor when it comes will it shame our trust. "When the desire cometh it shall be a tree of life."

Night is around us still; but it is not merely one of weeping, it is also one of watching. No sorrow is to make us less *watchful;* nay, much more. So far from tribulation throwing us off our guard, it should lead to added vigilance. It prevents our falling asleep, as we should certainly do were all peaceful and prosperous. It makes the night more cold and bitter to us, thereby rendering us more weary of it, and more eager for the day. Were the night air mild, and the night sky clear, we should grow contented with it, and cease to watch for day-break.

This is our night-watch. To this the Master has appointed us during His absence. "*Watch* ye therefore: for ye know not when the master of the house cometh, at even, or at midnight, or at the cock-crowing, or in the morning: lest coming suddenly he find you sleeping. And what I say unto you I say unto all, *Watch*" (Mark 13:35–37). It is the prospect of morning and of the Master's return that keeps us watching, especially in these last days, when watch after watch has come and gone, and He has not yet arrived. "His going forth is prepared as the morning" (Hos. 6:3); and that morning cannot now be distant.

The church must fulfill her night-watch. Whether long or short, perilous or easy, she must fulfill it. It is *watching* to which she is specially called; and sadly will she belie her profession, as well as disobey her Lord, if she *watches* not. She need not think to substitute other duties for this, as more needful, more important, or more in character. She dare not say, "I love, I believe, I pray, I praise, why should I also *watch*? Will not these do instead of watching, or is not watching included in these?" Her Lord has bidden her *watch*, and no other duty, no other grace, can be a substitute or an excuse for this.

She is to believe; but that is not all; she is also to *watch*. She is to rejoice; but that is not all; she is also to *watch*. She is to love; but that is not all; she is also to *watch*. She is to wait; but that is not all; she is also to *watch*. She is to long; but that is not all; she is also to *watch*. This is to be her special attitude, and nothing can compensate for it. By this she is to be known in all ages, as the watching one. By this the world is to be made to feel the difference between itself and her. By this she is specially to show how truly she feels herself to be a stranger here.

Men ask her, Why stand ye gazing up into heaven? Her reply is, "I am watching." Men taunt her, and say, Why this unrestfulness? Her reply is, "I am watching." Men think it strange that she runs not with them to the same excess of riot (1 Peter 4:4). She tells them, "I am watching." They ask her to come forth and join their gaiety, to come forth and sing their songs, to come forth and taste their pleasures, that thus they may teach her to forget her sorrows. She refuses, saying, "I dare not, I am watching." The scoffer mocks her, and says, Where is the promise of His coming? She heeds not, but continues watching, and clasps her hope more firmly.

Sometimes a feeble, doubting, or, it may be, inconsistent saint, asks in wonder, How are you so strong, so hardy, so able for the struggle, so successful in the battle? She answers, "I watch." Or he asks, How do you keep up a tone so elevated, and maintain a walk so close, so consistent, so unearthly? She answers, "I watch." Or he asks, How do you overcome sloth, and selfishness, and love of ease: or check fretfulness and anxiety, or gain the victory over a delaying spirit? She answers, "I watch." Or he asks, How do you make headway against your fears, and challenge danger, and defy enemies, and keep under the flesh? She replies, "I watch." Or he asks, How do you wrestle with your griefs, and dry up your tears, and heal your wounds, nay, glory in tribulation? She answers, "I watch."

Oh, what this watching can do, to one who understands it aright! Faith alone will not do. Love alone will not do. Expectation alone will not do. Obedience alone will not do. There must be *watching*.

And this watching takes for granted the suddenness and uncertainty of the day of the Lord. It does not say, the Lord must come in my day; but it says, the Lord may come in my day, therefore I must be on the outlook. This *may come* is the secret of a watchful spirit. Without it we cannot watch. We may love, and hope, and wait; but we cannot watch. Our lamps are to be always trimmed. Why? Not merely because the Bridegroom is to come, but because we know not *how soon* He may come. Our loins are to be *always* girt up. Why? Not simply because we know that there is to be a coming; but because we know not when that coming is to be.

The Lord foresaw the spirit of unwatchfulness into which His people would be apt to fall while He tarried, and He warns us against it. He would have us always to remember that there will be a danger of our becoming easy-minded and earthly-content with His absence instead of mourning because of it; content with His delay instead of joining in the primitive cry, "How long." He saw that the world would throw us off our guard; that few would really keep awake and watch; that many would get tired with watching, and find out excuses for not watching; that many would sit down and try to make themselves comfortable here without Him. Hence He so often repeated the warning—Watch! Hence He added, "lest coming suddenly he find you *sleeping.*"

His desire is, that we should be so watching, that when He cometh and knocketh, we may open unto Him *immediately* (Luke 12:36). And He pronounces a special blessing upon those servants whom He finds thus, promising that "he will gird himself, and make them sit down to meat, and will come forth and serve them." To be in such an attitude of watchfulness as that we shall be ready to open to Him *immediately,* is that to which He has promised so special a reward, so wondrous an honor. Ah, who among us is in this condition in these last days? Should we be ready to open to Him *immediately* were He arriving now? Should we not be thrown into confusion at the news of His coming, like servants unprepared for their master's return, and not counting on it so soon? Should we not have to be getting ready, when we should be opening the door? Should we not be running to put on our needful and proper raiment instead of going forth to welcome Him? Ah, what confusion in the household, what amazement, what fear, what bustle, what running to and fro, would there be in our day, were the tidings to be brought us, "the Lord has come!"

In the repeated command to *watch,* there is much of rebuke. The Lord could not trust us to remember it for ourselves, or obey unbidden. Had He been able to count on perfect love in us to Himself—love full and deep like His own, would He have thought of such a command? Would it have been needed? It would not. All that would have been needful would have been to tell us that He meant to return; love would have supplied the rest, and, of itself, have made us watchful; love would have made it impossible that it should be otherwise. It would have needed neither the command nor the declaration of uncertainty and suddenness. It would have anticipated all these. It would have acted upon them unbidden. But the Lord could not trust us. He could not trust our love; and therefore He adds the command, therefore He reiterates the warning. It is strange and sad indeed, that neither the power of love, nor the awe of the command, can quicken us into watchfulness or rouse us into preparation.

The announcements of the suddenness of His coming are very distinct and particular. There is nothing vague about them; nothing to take off the edge of the warning which they contain. They are much more specific and repeated than those of His first coming. His first advent took the church by surprise, even though He had set the time and numbered the years. How much more then is His second coming likely to surprise us, when, by the way in which He has announced it, He has prevented us from counting on any interval at all! Yet we watch not! Neither His measuring the time in the one case, nor His leaving it unmeasured in the other, produces the designed effect. "When the Son of man cometh, shall he find faith on the earth?"

During this our night-watch, faith is to be ever vigorous and in motion. For it is the root of watchfulness. Without faith one can hardly have the idea of what it is to watch. For all the objects towards which watchfulness turns are connected with things unseen—an unseen Savior, and an unseen kingdom.

When first we knew the Lord and believed on Him as the peace-maker, not only were we freely forgiven, but we were delivered from a present evil world. Things present fell off from us; things to come gathered around us. What was once shadowy became real, what once seemed real seemed then a shadow. Christ's words became real words; His truths real truths; His promises real promises. All else appeared unreal. The veil was not withdrawn, but we realized what was within it. The future did not become the present, nor the invisible the visible; but we felt as if they were so. Our faith was "the substance of things hoped for, the evidence of things not seen." Believing then that the Lord is coming, that the time is short, that the interval is uncertain, and that His arrival will be sudden, we *watch*. Unbelief throws us off our guard; but faith sends us to our watchtower. We know what our Lord meant when He said, "Blessed are they that have not seen and yet have believed."

Or, altering the words of our Lord, may we not also say, "Blessed are they that have seen and yet have *not* believed?" To see and yet *not* to believe, is one of the things that faith teaches us, and one of the things that quicken watchfulness. We look upon a world full of ungodliness and yet believe not that God has forsaken the earth. We see the world's wisdom worshipped, but yet believe not that it is wisdom. We see the power of evil, and yet believe not that evil shall triumph. We see confusion everywhere, and yet believe not but that order is God's law. We see a divided church, and yet believe that the church is one. We see mighty kingdoms ruling, and yet believe not that they shall abide. We see the saints trodden down, but yet believe not in their shame or extinction. We look upon the tomb of the righteous, and yet believe not that he is dead. We see the church's persecutions and defeats, and yet believe not only that she is conqueror, but invincible. We see the march of Antichrist, but yet believe not in his progress, save as a progress to doom. We see the world's joy, and yet believe not that it is joy. We see the saint's sorrow, and yet believe not that he is sorrowful. We see night, thick, deep night around us, but yet we believe not in the night, but in the day.

Thus faith triumphs. We believe, we trust, we hope; and so doing, we stand above the world. We lift up our eyes to the hills whence cometh our help. We look towards the east, where the dawn breaks. We *watch* for the morning. Our night-watch has been long and weary; but the morning will soon end it. The watching, the waiting, and the hoping will then be done, but the loving will be for ever.

We *watch;* for we know of no interval between us and the Lord's appearing. The hour of our meeting with Him, and with those whom we have loved and lost, may be nigh at hand. Sooner than we think, we may be joined together inseparably, our bodies clothed with resurrection-health, and our souls rejoicing in holiness and love.

We watch; for it is night, and though we are not children of the night, still the night with its shadows rests heavily upon us, making us with wistful keenness to look out for its passing away. We grow more dissatisfied with it as it deepens. It brings so many griefs, it gathers round us so many temptations, it calls up so many dangers, it gives courage to so many enemies, that we grow troubled at its lasting so long. Yet we cannot shake it off. God's purpose must be served, and His time must run out. Till then let us possess our souls in patience, whilst watching for day-spring, and stirring up our souls with the assurance that we know of nothing between us and the ending of our long night-watch.

We watch; for the day is ours, with all that it contains of gladness and sunshine. We are weary of the night, and we rejoice that it is not ours, though we are in it; but that the day is ours. Just as we can say, "the kingdom is ours," so we can say, "the day is ours." And we watch for it as being ours. Its light is ours; its blue sky is ours; its mild air is ours; its cheerful sounds are ours; its friendly greetings are ours; all that it calls forth of joy, and health, and purity are ours. Need any wonder that we should watch for such a day?

We watch; for the night is far spent. Not only do we know of nought before us ere the Lord arrives; but we know of much behind us. Hours, years, ages have gone by. And if the whole night was to be brief, only a "little while," then surely very much of it must now be over. "The night is far spent," says the apostle; literally, it is "cut off," it is *foreshortened,* that is, it is becoming shorter, it is drawing to a close. Behind us are lying centuries of tears and shadows; the greater part of the little while *must* be past; the day *must* be at hand. The nearness makes the thought of day doubly welcome. We bend towards it with warm longings; we strain our eyes to catch the first token of it; we rouse ourselves to vigilance, knowing that now is our salvation nearer than when we believed.

How it disappoints, how it damps, to be told, there are centuries more of this night-watching still to come! Could that be proved, it would sadly chill our hope. We might at once come down from our watch-tower and give up our expectations. To "look for and haste unto the coming of the day of God," would be no longer a duty. The last generation of the church, living at the close of the millennium, might get up into the watch-tower, but for us, watching would be a name, a mere attitude of form or show.

It has ever been Satan's object to interpose some object between the church and her Lord's arrival; but never did he light upon a more specious, more successful device than that of making the interposed object a glorious and blessed one. To no other would the church have listened. She would have shrunk and turned away from a thousand years' sorrow; but she is attracted and dazzled by the promise of a thousand years' rest and joy. Yet, is the interposition of any fixed interval (be it sad or joyous), lawful or scriptural? If the Lord's advent be thrust into the distance, it matters not what may be introduced to fill the interval. If the Hope of the church be hidden, it is of small moment whether it be by a shroud of sackcloth or by a veil of woven gold.

God deals with the church as one. Though consisting of many generations, He looks upon it as one body. And in reference to her hope, He has so framed His revelation, that every generation of the church should stand upon the same footing as the last. How has this been done? How has the first age, and how have all subsequent ages, been placed in the same position as the last? Simply by concealing the interval. In this thing it has been truly "the glory of God to conceal a matter" (Prov. 25:2). For by this method, so simple and so natural, each age of the church has been made to feel, precisely as the last will feel—to watch, just as the last will watch, when the Lord is in very deed at hand. And thus that body which is spread over centuries, has at all times been made to occupy a position and present a character, the same as if it had been a body whose life and actings were summed up in one generation. So that any known interval interposed before the advent, alters the posture, destroys the character, and breaks the oneness of the church, while it defeats the object which God had so specially in view in keeping the times and seasons in His own power.

Often, since the Lord left the earth, has the watch been changed and the guard relieved. God has not tried too sorely the faith of any one age by making the watch too long. In mercy he has cut down man's age from patriarchal longevity to three-score years and ten, lest the over-wearied watchers should sink under the toil and hardship. It is this that makes unwatchfulness so inexcusable. Adam, or Seth, or Methuselah, or Noah, might have had the edge of their watchfulness blunted by the long conflict of nine hundred years; but what excuse have we for heedlessness! Our time of service is brief, and to fall asleep or grow impatient, would indicate sad indolence and unfaithfulness. "What! could ye not watch with me one hour? watch and pray, lest ye enter into temptation," If the Lord come not in our day, by His personal presence to end our watching, we still cannot complain of over-endurance or exhaustion, seeing we shall be so soon relieved and taken into His nearer presence, there to watch in rest and joy and light, as here we have watched in weariness and grief and darkness.

3

The Earnests of the Morning

The true morning has not yet broken; hardly does it give forth any sign of breaking, save the deeper darkness that is the sure foreteller of the dawn.

It is still night upon the *earth;* and "the children of the night" are going to and fro in the world's streets, doing "the unfruitful works of darkness"; "walking in lasciviousness, lusts, excess of wine, revellings, banquetings, and abominable idolatries"; yielding to the "flattering lips" of the seducer, that "lieth in wait at every corner" in "the black and dark night" (Prov. 7:9–21); making "provision for the flesh," by "living in rioting and drunkenness, in chambering and wantonness, in strife and envying" (Rom. 13:13); compassing themselves about with sparks of their own kindling, which only sadden the gloom and make us feel more truly that it is night.

It is still night to the *church;* a night of danger, a night of weariness, a night of weeping. Her firmament is dark and troubled. The promise of morning is sure, and she is looking out for it with fixed and pleading eye, sore tried with the long gloom, yet it has not arisen. It is still deferred—deferred in mercy to an unready world, to whom the ending of this night shall be the closing of hope, and the sealing of ruin, and the settling down of the infinite darkness. "For the Lord is not slack concerning his promise, as some men count slackness, but is long-suffering to us-ward, not willing that any should perish, but that all should come to repentance" (2 Peter 3:9).

But though it is *night,* there are times both in the saint's own history and the church's annals, which may be spoken of as *mornings* even now. Such was the "morning" to Adam when Seth was born to him after Abel's death (Gen. 4:25). Such was the "morning" to Noah when the flood dried up, and the face of the earth was renewed. Such was the "morning" to Jacob when the tidings came to him that Joseph was yet alive. Such was the "morning" to Naomi when Ruth and Boaz wiped off the tears of widowhood, and when in her old age she "saw her seed," and "took the child and laid it in her bosom" (Ruth 4:16). Such was Hannah's "morning" when, after long years of bitterness, "the Lord granted her petition," and "she went her way and was no more sad" (1 Sam. 1:18). Such was the "morning" that dawned on Job when the Lord accepted him, and turned his captivity, giving him twice as much as he had before, "blessing his latter end more than his beginning." Such was Israel's "morning" when the Lord turned back the captivity of Zion, "making them like men that dream," filling "their mouth with laughter and their tongue with singing," in the day of their deliverance from exile.

Thus there are "mornings" ever and anon bursting on us now. They are indeed little more than brief brightenings of the darkness—lulls in the long tempest that is to rage unspent till the Lord come. Still we may call them "mornings," just as we give the name of midday to the dim kindlings of the sky at daily noon, in the six months' arctic night, when the sun keeps below the horizon. Or better and truer, we may call them *earnests of the morning*—that morning which is to outshine all mornings, and to swallow up alike the darkness and the light of a present evil world. Dim and transient as are these earnests, they are unutterably gladdening. They cheer the heavy darkness and are pledges of sun-rise.

Our life on earth, "the life that we now live in the flesh," is thus made up of many nights and many mornings. It is not all one night, nor is it all one day. Everything pertaining to it seems to revolve or alternate. It is a life of sinking and rising, of going and returning, of ebbing and flowing, of shade and brightness. The health of the soul seems in some measure to need such changes, just as the soil owes much of its fruitfulness to the vicissitudes of the seasons.

As there is no even continuance of constant good, so there is no equal pressure of unbroken evil. As the season of calm is brief, so is the burst of the storm. The days of darkness are many—more in number than the days of light, yet they do not last always. "Many are the afflictions of the righteous," yet there are *breaks* in the line of evil, for it is added, "the Lord delivereth him out of them all."

Our God has so fashioned us, and so regulated our circumstances, that each grief has its crisis, its spring-tide, after which it seems, as if by a law, to recede. Not only can the soul not bear beyond a fixed amount of pain or pressure without giving way, but it cannot be kept too long upon the stretch. If the tension is protracted, the "spirit fails," the mind breaks down. Or if this is not the case, callousness comes on; we grow stupid and insensible. Affliction loses its power by being too heavy or too long.

The highest mountain has its summit, the deepest mine-shaft has its lowest level. Nor, in general, are these long in being reached. So even when there is sorrow upon sorrow, there is respite between, or gladness at the close of the dark series. The outer and the inner world have, to some extent, the same laws of alternation and relief. Tides and variations seem needful in both. Thus it was in the life of David. At one time he stood with gladness in the courts of his God; at another he bemoaned himself, saying, "When shall I come and appear before God?" At one time he went with the multitude; at another he wandered in solitude and exile. At one time he kept holy day with the thousands of Israel, joining in the voice of joy and praise; at another his tears were his meat day and night. At one time his soul was cast down and disquieted within him; at another time he praised Jehovah as the health of his countenance. At one time he could look with open eye upon the glory of Jehovah in His house; at another he could only remember Him from the land of Jordan and of the Hermonites, from the hill Mizar. At one time deep called unto deep, all God's waves went over him; at another the Lord commanded His loving kindness and opened his mouth in song. Such were the tides of David's history—the vicissitudes of day and night in his varying course. True type of every saint's history, not only in the old age of shadows, but in our own! True example of the changes and tossings marked out for the church in her course on earth from shame to glory! What else are we to look for till the Lord come? In the first age of the church, in the time of righteous Abel, it was so. "The evening and the morning were the first day." In the last age of the church, just ere the second Adam is brought in, it shall be no less so. "The evening and the morning were the sixth day." Then comes the world's seventh and brightest day—a day of cloudless splendor, unbroken and unending.

How wise, how gracious that it should be so! One firmament of gloom, spanning our whole life-time, would be intolerable. One long heavy chain of grief, with which we could never get familiar, and on which we could never learn to look calmly; or one linked succession of griefs, ever tearing open old wounds and adding new ones, would wither up existence and blight life before its prime. Man's nature could not bear it; man's heart would sink under it, unless made totally callous by some unnatural process, or sustained by daily miracle; in which case grief would cease to be grief, and there could be no such thing as trial or chastisement at all.

Hence, He who "knoweth our frame and remembereth that we are dust," not only "stayeth his rough wind in the day of his east wind;" but often, for a season, bids both be still, and breathes on us only with the freshness of the mild south. For thus has He spoken, "I will not contend for ever, neither will I be always wroth; for the spirit should fail before me, and the souls which I have made" (Isa. 57:16). Such then is God's purpose concerning us, and such His reasons for it. The purpose is a gracious and a tender one; no less so are the reasons for it. He tells us, that though He does, at seasons, contend with us, yet He will not prolong the contest beyond a certain time or limit; for in such a strife, who could stand before the Mighty One? "In measure when it shooteth forth thou wilt debate with it" (Isa. 27:8); that is, He will set bounds to the sorrow and the smiting which cannot be over-passed; He will say to them, even in their fiercest course, "Thus far shalt thou go, and no farther." For were He to allow that tide to roll on unhindered, who, even of His own chosen and beloved ones, could withstand its rush, or sustain themselves amid its deepening waters?

Yet let us not forget what the sorrow has done for us while it lasted; and what the night has been, though dark and sad.

It has been a night of grief, yet a night of blessing; a night in which there may have been many things which we could wish forgotten, yet many more which we should wish to be remembered for ever. Often, during its gloom, we called it "wearisome," and said. "When shall I arise and the night be gone?" (Job 7:4). Yet how much was there to reconcile us to it; nay, to fill us with praise because of it! It was then that the Lord drew near, and the world was displaced, and self was smitten, and our will conquered, and faith grew apace, and hope became brighter and more eager, and the things that are unseen were felt to be the real and the true; Jerusalem that is above was seen by us as our proper home.

It was then that we had "songs in the *night*" (Ps. 42:8). Our "reins instructed us in the *night* seasons" (Ps. 16:7). It was "in the night that we remembered the name" of our God (Ps. 119:55), and "desired him with our souls" (Isa. 26:9), "meditating on him in the night-watches" (Ps. 63:6). It was "in the *night*" that "he led us with a light of fire" (Ps. 78:14). It was in the night that "the dew lay upon our branch" (Job 29:19), and with the dew there came down the manna; for the manna and the dew fell together (Num. 11:9), so that out of the bosom of the darkness there came at once nourishment and freshness. It was then that we were taught sympathy with a groaning creation, taking part in its "earnest expectation," and waiting for resurrection even as it is looking out for restitution; it was then that we were taught to know our high office, as those who have the first-fruits of the Spirit, "to lead (as one has written) the choir of all-complaining nature"; for it was then that the Spirit's power came forth upon us to tune the chords of our manifold being, that they might give forth the true note of mingled hope and sadness, peculiar to creation in its present low estate; and when we were fretting under the touch, and perhaps, with sentimental weakness, talking of broken strings and a blighted life, the hand of the great Master-tuner was upon us, giving to each rebellious chord its proper tension, that from the re-tuned instrument there might come forth that special harmony which He desires to draw from it in this present age—that special harmony by which He is to be glorified on earth, until Eden comes again and the wilderness blossoms as the rose.

It was then that we could make the utterance of Jacob's patient faith our own, "I have waited for thy salvation, O Lord;" subscribing ourselves to our fellow saints as "your companion in tribulation and in the kingdom and patience of Christ" (that is, in patient waiting for His kingdom). It was then that these words of blessed cheer fell so sweetly on our ears, "He who testifieth these things saith, Surely I come quickly," drawing forth from our lips the glad response,

"Even so, come, Lord Jesus." And it was then that, while learning thus to plead "make haste," we also learned to say with the Bride, "A bundle of myrrh is my well-beloved unto me, he shall lie all night in my bosom" (Song 1:13).

Blessed and profitable, however, as we have found the night with its still seclusion and solemn teachings, it is not the morning nor the day. And its very darkness makes us long the more for the anticipated sunrise—for "the flight of shadows and the eternal day break."

Nor are we hindered from desiring the day. Impatience is forbidden, but not desire. Let us possess our souls in patience, for he is neither the brave nor the believing man who says, "Let me die, for the cup is bitterer than I can drink;" but he who under the sorest grief can say, "Let me live on and be useful, whatever may be the bitterness of the cup." But still we may long for the ending of the night. As in sickness we may long for health, and put forth all fit means for its attainment; so in darkness we may cry earnestly for the dawning, especially because we know that God has a day in store for us after the night is done—a day which is to be far more than a compensation for all previous sorrow. For every night God has provided a morning, so that as we have many nights, we have also many mornings here. They are not indeed "mornings without clouds," but still they are mornings whose cheering light lifts up the heavy spirit and brightens the faded eye.

But for the world, the children of the night, the heedless, the pleasure-loving world, what morning is there, or what earnest of the morning? None. Or at least it deserves not the name of morning. Their "sorrows are multiplied," because they have hastened after other gods. Their joy is but a moment. Their consolation is no better than a dream. They serve a god that cannot save, and that cannot comfort. Their portion here at the best is emptiness; and the end is the eternal blackness and the infinite despair. The tidings of God's free love they heed not; but the tidings of His wrath they shall ere long be made to heed; if now they turn not to Him who is entreating of them this one favor, that they would bring their sins to Him for pardon, and let Him bear all their griefs and carry all their sorrows.

4

The Use of These Earnests

"Now for a swifter race!" was the resolve of one over whose path sorrow was beginning to darken heavily. "Now for a busier and more useful life!" was the utterance of another, as he rose from his knees, after pouring out the bitterness of his grief into the ear of God.

In these cases tribulation was taking its true course and working its right end. It had gone down to the most sacred depths of the renewed heart, and was calling up buried feelings of devotedness that had remained dormant, but not extinct, under a mass of worldliness. It smote our selfishness, our narrow-mindedness, our sloth, our flesh-pleasing, and reminded us that we had no time to loiter or to sleep. Tearing off the veil which prosperous days had flung over our eyes, it pointed to the vanity of things "seen and temporal," till the vastness of the unseen and the eternal so grew upon us, that we rose up and went forth, resolving on a swifter race and a busier life on earth.

Still there was a hindrance. The very trial that stirred us up also weighed us down, unknitting our strength, and causing us well nigh to faint. The pressure staid our swiftness, and the deep wound, still bleeding, enfeebled us. We sought to run, but were often held back; and when we would have gone forth to do the work of God, we were constrained to turn aside and go alone, that, in weeping and pleading, we might relieve our heavy hearts. We may at times seem to escape from the sorrow, and, in the fire of zeal, almost forget its bitterness; yet it returns to us in full strength, and we feel as if a chain were on our limbs. There is not indeed the bondage arising from any uncertainty as to the relationship in which we stand towards God. These fetters fell from us when we received God's record of forgiving love, and knew what it is to be freely pardoned. These fetters no amount of trial can reimpose on us, if "we hold the beginning of our confidence stedfast unto the end." Nay, it is often in a day of grief that we realize most blessedly how completely grace has set us free. But though there is no re-placement of our chains, and no bitterness of bondage again tasted, still chastisement is "not joyous but grievous"; and "being grievous" it sometimes disheartens and disables us, so that we cannot do the same amount of service, or undergo the same degree of toil for God, as otherwise we might have done. At the *first* lighting down of the stroke this is always felt, for we are men in the flesh, and the flesh gives way. "The spirit truly is willing, but the flesh is weak." And for a considerable time this continues to be experienced; shorter or longer, according to our natural characters, or according to the specialties of the trial.

Hence it is that affliction is often more a season of preparation for service than a time of actual service, save only as *patience* is service, for "they also serve who only stand and wait." Let us not fret, then, nor be cast down, because we feel disabled for zealous service for a time. Let it suffice us to know that we are preparing for this. And when the load is lifted off or becomes lighter, *then* we run with speedier foot, *then* we labor with fuller strength and freer heart. We cannot expect to be wholly free from sorrow here, for some amount of trial is always needful to keep us from forgetting that this is not our rest—that this is the night and not the day; but still these intervals of calm and sunshine are precious times—

times of blessing; times of service; times for the swift race and the busy life.

These mornings here, coming after the nights that thicken over us, are most profitable. They not only relieve the "o'er-fraught heart," but are seasons in which we find leisure to learn lessons of wisdom and holiness, which in the time of the sorrow we had overlooked or put from us. The returning elasticity of spirit enables us to rise from our depression, now that the weight has in some measure been lifted off. Too continuous a pressure of grief is apt to make us moody, selfish, desponding, slothful. It narrows the circle alike of vision and of sympathy, and dries up the springs of our nature. But when peace returns after a season of trouble, we seem doubly fitted as well as nerved for duty. The trial has sobered and mellowed us. It has taught us to endure hardness as good soldiers of Jesus Christ. It has rubbed off excrescences. It has made us less selfish, less contracted in soul. It has taught us to look round with sympathy upon a suffering world and a weeping church. It was as if we had been taken aside for a season into some quiet nook or dark cave, from which, while alone and undistracted, we could look out unobserved upon the multitudes that passed and repassed. And having been thus brought to form truer, riper judgments, we are led forth again to act—to act more unselfishly, more zealously, yet more stedfastly and soberly.

Our life, after a night of trial has passed over us, should be a life of truer aims, of steadier walk, of higher level, of keener, purer vision. If not, we have suffered in vain.

During the night, much was of necessity hidden from us. But the morning discloses what the night had hidden. It shows us how desperate the struggle was between us and our God, of which at the time we were hardly aware. It shows the amount of patience, love, and faithfulness, that have been expended on us by God. It shows the extent of the evil in us which had drawn down the chastening. It puts us in a position for bringing into practice the knowledge of the world's vanity and wretchedness which sorrow had taught us. Thus the morning carries out the lessons of the night, and gives us opportunity for exemplifying them. And thus the alternation of trial and rest which makes up our lot on earth, is in truth but a succession of lessons, and of opportunities for practicing them. "Day unto day uttereth speech, and night unto night showeth knowledge" (Ps. 19:2).

Thus trial prepares for service. It nerves us, it braces us for toil. It shows us what alone is worth living for, so that when the force of it is in some measure abated, we find ourselves ready to start anew for the race, ready to wield the weapons of our warfare with a firmer and more skilful hand.

These intervals of brightness, then, are the true seasons for labor. These earnests of the morning should be prized as opportunities specially afforded us by God for strenuous labor. If thus laid out, how blessed will they be found! They are brief, for tribulation is our lot on earth, not ease; but this should only arouse to new vigor; for if they be thus brief, we have no moments to idle away.

But it is here that so many stumble. In trial they call upon the Lord and vow their life to Him. Through evil report and good they will follow Him; on the rough way or the smooth they will walk with Him; by labor, by sacrifice, by watchfulness, by costly gifts, they will prove their love, and zeal, and constancy! Good words and sincerely spoken! But so were the words of the disciple, "If I should die with thee, I will not deny thee in any wise." He spoke what he truly felt, but when the hour came, the resolution was not to be found. So with us. Trial calls forth many a high thought and prompts to noble purposes. Yet how seldom do these thoughts ripen; how often do these purposes die! Peace returns, sunshine brightens over us, our broken strength knits again, and we sink back into sloth! The calm hour for which we longed, that we might do something for God, has come, but it finds us nearly as heedless and selfish as before we entered into the storm.

This must not be. Why were we smitten, but just that we might be stirred up? And why were we delivered, but just that we might work more strenuously, more efficaciously? How sad, then, that both the trial and the enlargement should fail of their purposed end!

These times of enlargement are times of light and gladness. In these mornings joy has come to us. It is not the mere reaction from sorrow; it is not mere familiarity with suffering; it is not oblivion of the past; it is not the calm of over-spent feeling. It is joy from the Lord. And "the joy of the Lord is our strength." He who gave us the night has given us also the morning. He who called up the storm has brought back the calm. So that it is His *joy* in which we rejoice; and this joy is our strength. Let not this strength lie idle. The calm will not last; the clouds will soon return; and it concerns us to lay out well the brief hour of light. "I must work the works of him that sent me while it is day; the night cometh when no man can work" (John 9:4).

5

The Morning-Star

It was "very early in the morning," while "it was yet dark," that Jesus rose from the dead. Not the sun, but only the morning-star, shone upon His opening tomb. The shadows had not fled, the citizens of Jerusalem had not awoke. It was still night — the hour of sleep and of darkness, when He arose. Nor did His rising break the slumbers of the city.

So it shall be "very early in the morning," when "it is yet dark," and when nought but the morning-star is shining, that Christ's body, the church, shall arise. Like Him, His saints shall awake when the children of the night and darkness are still sleeping their sleep of death. In their arising they disturb no one. The world hears not the voice that summons them, or if it hears, shall only say, "It thunders," as did the unbelieving Jews when the Father's voice responded to the prayer of Jesus (John 12:29). As Jesus laid them quietly to rest, each in his own still tomb, like children in the arms of their mother; so as quietly, as gently, shall He awake them when the hour arrives.

He is the Morning-star. "I am the root and offspring of David, the bright and morning-star" (Rev. 22:16). And this name is given to Him not only because of the glory of His person and the brightness of His appearing, but because of the *time* when He is to appear.

The first act, at His appearing, when He comes in glory,

the first indication of His arrival, while yet aloft "in the air," is likened to the shining of the morning-star. Afterwards He shall come forth as "the Sun of righteousness," filling the whole earth with His brightness, and shadowing the nations with His healing wings (Mal. 4:2); but at first He shows Himself as the Morning-star—big with the hope of day, yet not the day; brighter than other stars and eclipsing all of them, yet not the Day-star; forerunner of the sun, yet not the sun; foreteller of the dawn, yet not the dawn.

Hence His promise to the conqueror is, "I will give him the morning-star" (Rev. 2:28); that is, I will give Myself to him as the morning-star; I will show Myself to him as such; I will confer on him this pre-eminence, this special blessedness.

We read in Scripture of "the eye-lids of the morning;" and the morning-star is the first beam shooting from under these lids as they begin to re-open, that the eye of day may again irradiate the earth. It is only they who awake early that see the first opening of these eyelids, or gaze upon the morning-star, or breathe the morning freshness, or taste the morning dew. So it is with those of whom it is said, "Blessed and holy is he that hath part in the first resurrection." To them come the quickening words, "Awake and sing, ye that dwell in dust" (Isa. 26:19). Into their tomb the earliest ray of glory finds its way. They drink in the first gleams of morning, while as yet the eastern clouds give but the faintest signs of its uprising. Its genial fragrance, its soothing stillness, its bracing freshness, its sweet loneliness, its quiet purity, all so solemn and yet so full of hope, these are theirs. Oh, the contrast between these things and the dark night through which they have passed! Oh, the contrast between these things and the grave from which they have sprung! And as they skate off the encumbering turf, flinging mortality aside, and rising, in glorified bodies, to meet their Lord in the air, they are lighted and guided upward, along the untrained pathway, by the beams of that Star of morning, which, like the star of Bethlehem, conducts them to the presence of the King.

There seem to be more *periods* than one (if times so very brief may be called by that name) opening out upon us when the Lord comes. Just as there are more *scenes* than one, and more *acts* than one, in "the day of the Lord," so there are more periods than one. And it is interesting to notice these in connection with the morning-star.

All the time up to the moment of His appearing is reckoned *night*. Then the scenes change, and, step by step, the day with its full sunshine is brought in. First, there is the *period of the Morning-star*, during which the dead saints awake and the living saints are changed; then that which is sown in corruption is raised in incorruption, that which is sown in dishonor is raised in glory, that which is sown in weakness is raised in power, that which is sown a natural body is raised a spiritual body; and then they that have long dwelt in dust awake and sing. In every land they have found a grave, and every land now gives up the sleeping clay. They come forth "in the beauties of holiness from the womb of the morning," like the ten thousand times ten thousand dew-drops of the night, made visible by the morning-star, and sparkling to its far-coming glory (Ps. 110:3; Isa. 26:19). It is long since "*light* was sown for the righteous" (Ps. 97:11), and this is the first-fruits of the harvest.

Next there is the *period of the twilight*. This is the time when "the light shall not be clear nor dark," like "the morning spread upon the mountains" (Joel 2:2). Then has the last battle-strife begun; then the Lord with His rod of iron is breaking His enemies in pieces like a potter's vessel; then He cometh forth from His place to punish the inhabitants of the earth for their iniquity; then, with all His saints, He executes the infinite vengeance, delivers Israel, destroys Antichrist, lays waste the world with sore calamity and purging fire. "Before the morning he is not," says the prophet, foretelling the ruin of the great enemy of Israel and the church (Isa. 17:14).

Next there is the morning. The enemy has disappeared; each wreck that marked either his dominion or his destruction is gone. The face of the earth is renewed, the storm is laid to rest, and the glory of an unclouded sun and an unsullied firmament makes creation sing for joy. The voice of the Beloved is heard, "Rise up, my love, my fair one, and come away. For, lo, the winter is past, the rain is over and gone; the flowers appear on the earth; the time of the singing of birds is come, and the voice of the turtle is heard in our land; the fig tree putteth forth her green figs, and the vines with the tender grape give a good smell. Arise, my love, my fair one, and come away" (Song 2:10–13).

Lastly, there is the day in its full brightness. For the path of this Just One is like a shining light that shineth more and more unto the perfect day. Of that day, earth has never seen the like. For that day it waits in patient hope, struggling hard, meanwhile, with darkness, and laboring to throw off its long sad weight of ill.

It is as if the glory of the Lord, when first coming within sight of the earth, showed itself in the far distance, as the star of morning; token most welcome and hopeful, recognized at once by those who knew the true light of the world, and who had often in other days looked out wistfully for the Star of Jacob. It is, *next,* as if the same glory, when it neared the earth, showed itself in terrible majesty as the sign of the Son of man, in seeing which all the tribes of the earth mourn (Matt. 24:30; Rev. 1:7); for just as *in the morning-watch* the Lord looked through the pillar of fire and cloud and troubled the host of the Egyptians, (Ex. 14:24) so, when He cometh with clouds, "all kindreds of the earth shall wail because of him." It is, next, as if the same glory of the Son of man, coming still nearer, took up its destined position, and spread its skirts over earth as did the pillar-cloud over the tents of

Israel. It is, *lastly,* as if this glory, this more than Shekinah-splendor, showed itself as the Sun of righteousness, bearing healing in His wings, wherewith He heals the *nations,* so that the inhabitant shall no more say, I am sick; wherewith He heals the *earth,* so that the curse takes flight; wherewith He heals the air, so that it poisons no more. Then day shall utter speech to day in a way unheard of before; then shall their line go throughout all the earth, and their words to the end of the world, when out of that "tabernacle which he doth set for the Sun," that Sun shall come forth as a bride-groom out of his chamber, rejoicing as a strong man to run a race. Then shall come to pass the saying that is written, "Behold, the glory of the God of Israel came from the way of the east, and his voice was like the noise of many waters, and the earth shined with his glory" (Ezek. 43:2).

With all of these in succession the saints have to do, from the time that they are roused out of their tombs by the first beams of the Morning-star, to have part in the first resurrection. But it is only the first of these that we are now considering.

The promise "to him that overcometh" is, "I will give him the morning-star" (Rev. 2:28). Of all the blessings symbolized or indicated by that star, he is made partaker. The first streak of dawn is his. He is summoned from the dust to meet the morning ere yet one ray of it has touched the earth. The first glimpse of the long-waited-for glory his eye shall see, when other eyes abide in darkness. In this first token of a coming Lord, his soul shall rejoice. At this, the first sound of the returning Bridegroom's voice, he shall go forth with ready love. The first object that shall meet his eye on awaking from the tomb, shall be the Star of Jacob.

This earnest of creation's better day is the portion of the saints. The deliverance of creation is at hand. The time of "the manifestation of the sons of God" is come. Now, arrayed in light, themselves the sons of light, they shall shine as the brightness of the firmament and as the stars for ever and ever. Now, transformed into the image of the Morning-star—themselves the stars of morning, they prepare to sing together over the new creation, when its foundations shall be fastened and its corner-stone laid by Him who is to make all things new. Death is now swallowed up of victory; the grave is rifled; the spoiler is spoiled; ashes are exchanged for beauty; the light that was quenched is rekindled; the sorrow passes into joy; and the darkness of a brief night ends in the uprising of the endless day.

As for those that "are alive and remain unto the coming of the Lord," though they shall not go before those that are asleep, yet they shall not be behind them in the blessedness. They shall have the same privileges of the early morning—the same honor, the same glory. Their eye shall look upon that Star; and it shall be to them all that it is to those who were "dwelling in dust." Living in the last days of a God-denying world—days dark and hateful as those of Noah or of Lot—their righteous souls vexed from day to day with wickedness "that cannot rest," "casting up its mire and dirt" on every side—danger pressing, conflict thickening, persecution assailing, sorrows multiplying—how welcome shall that sign be to them, springing up like hope when all is hopeless, and fore-tokening life, refreshment, rest, gladness, to the troubled and despairing earth!

Like the anxious watchman on some fortress, they have been wearying for the morning, and it has come at last! Like the belated traveler, pressing on over hill and moor and rock and waste and thicket, they have been seeking at every turn to catch the light of their cottage window, and it is seen at last! Like the tempest-tossed apostle, when neither sun nor stars for many days appeared, "they wish for day," and are glad beyond measure at the tokens of its approach. The glimmer of the light-house has hitherto been their comfort and their guide. By it they have shaped their way and cheered their hearts. But, of a sudden, the beacon seems to sink away, and ere they are aware, its light is lost amid the far-outrivalling brightness of the Morning-star.

But upon the unready and unwatching world that Star rises with no ray of blessing. It rises only to shed "disastrous blight," and give token of the desolations that are at hand. For when Noah entered the ark the flood burst forth, or as when Lot entered Zoar the fire came down, so when the saints are caught up then the wrath is poured out and the door is shut.

Till then the gate of peace stands wide open, and into the chambers of safety all are beckoned. The most unready of all the children of men may go freely in; for the grace that invites makes no exceptions, but welcomes the unworthiest. It would fain allure the seekers of vain joy, from joys that are so vain. It would fain win the heart of the sorrowful, who mourn and yet have no comforter, because they have no God. It would fain draw in the secure into a place of true safety, ere the storm arise that is to break in pieces the strong foundations of the earth.

Children of the earth—you especially whose sorrows are multiplied, and whose hearts are sick with disappointment— give heed to the gracious warning! Enter the hiding-place and be safe for ever. Thrice blessed are those griefs and disappointments that lead you out of lying refuges into the sure covert from the storm, that call you from the joy of the world into the joy of God.

6

The Morning

The watchman said, "The morning cometh" (Isa. 21:12); and though, while making this answer, he forewarns us of night, he also assures us of morning. There is a morning, says he, therefore do not give way to faintness of spirit; but there is a night between, therefore take warning: that you may not be surprised nor dismayed, as if the promise were broken, or some strange thing allowed to befall you.

There may be delay, he intimates, before the morning—a dark delay, for which we should be prepared. During this he calls to watchfulness: for the length of the night is hidden, the time of daybreak is left uncertain. We must be on the outlook, with our eyes fixed on the eastern hills. We have nothing wherewith to measure the hours, save the sorrows of the church and the failing of hearts.

During this delay the watchman encourages us to "inquire," to "return," to "come." He expects us to ask "how long," and say, "When will the night be done?" He takes for granted that such will be the proceeding of men who really long for morning. To the hills of Seir they will again and again return, to learn from the watchman what is the promise of day. For no familiarity with the night can ever reconcile them to its darkness, or make morning less desirable and welcome.

It is right for us to desire the morning, to hope for it, to weary for it, to inquire as to the signs of it hour after hour.

God has set this joy before us, and it were strange indeed if, when compassed about with so many sorrows, we could forget it, or be heedless as to its arrival. For the coming of the morning is the coming of Him whom we long to see. It is the coming of Him "who turneth the shadow of death into the morning" (Amos 5:8). It is the return of Him whose absence has been night, and whose presence will be day. It is the return of Him who is the resurrection and the life, and who brings resurrection with Him; the return of Him who is creation's Lord, and who brings with Him deliverance to creation; the return of Him who is the church's Head, and who brings with Him triumph and gladness to His church.

All the joy, the calm, the revivifying freshness of the morning are wrapped up in Him. When He appears, day appears, life appears, fruitfulness appears. The curse departs. The "bondage of corruption" is no more. Clouds, storms, troubles, sorrows vanish. The face of nature reassumes the smile of unfallen times. It is earth's festival, the world's jubilee. "The heavens rejoice, the earth is glad, the sea roars and the fullness thereof, the fields are joyful and all that is therein, the trees of the wood rejoice, the floods clap their hands, and the hills are joyful together before the Lord; for He has come, for He has come to judge the earth; with righteousness shall he judge the world, and the people with his truth" (Ps. 96:11; 98:7).

This morning has been long anticipated. Age after age it has attracted the church's eye, and fixed her hope. On the promise of it her faith has been resting, and towards the hastening of it her prayers have gone forth. Though afar off, it has been descried, and rejoiced in as the sure consummation towards which all things are moving forward according to the Father's purpose. "There is a morning" has been the word of consolation brought home to the burdened heart of many a saint when ready to say, with David, "I am desolate," or with Jeremiah, "He hath set me in dark places as they that be dead of old."

Let us dwell for a little on some of these Old Testament allusions to the morning. Let us take first the 30th Psalm.

David had been in sorrow, and in coming out of it he makes known to the saints his consolations: "Sing unto the Lord, O ye saints of his, and give thanks at the remembrance of his holiness. For his anger endureth but a moment; in his favour is life: weeping may endure for a night, but joy cometh in the morning" (Ps. 30:4, 5). The earnest of that morning he had already tasted, but the morning itself he anticipates. Then joy has come. Then he can say (verse 11), "Thou hast turned for me my mourning into dancing: thou hast put off my sackcloth, and girded me with gladness." But it is the voice of a greater than David that is heard in this psalm. It is one of Christ's resurrection psalms, like the eighteenth and the 116th. He was "lifted up," so that His foes were not made to rejoice over Him. He cried, and was "healed." His "soul was brought up from the grave." There was anger against Him "for a moment," when as the sinner's substitute He bore the sinner's curse. But in Jehovah's favor there was "life." He had a night of weeping, a night of "strong crying and tears," when His soul was "sorrowful even unto death," and when beneath the waves of that sorrow He sunk, commending His spirit into the Father's hands. But it was a night no more. Morning came, and with morning, joy. Coming forth from the tomb, He left all His sorrow behind: His sackcloth was put off, and He arose "girded with gladness." He found morning and joy; and He is "the first-fruits of them that slept." His rising was the rising of His saints. There was a morning for Him, therefore there shall be one for us—a morning bright with resurrection-glory.

Let us next take Psalm 49. These are Christ's words, as is proved from the quotation of verse 4 in Matthew 13:35. He summons the whole world to listen. He "speaks of wisdom,"

for He is Wisdom. He points to the vanity of riches, and
their insufficiency to redeem a soul; and who knew so well
as He what a ransom was needed? He sees men going on
in their wickedness, self-confidence, and vain-glory. He
proclaims their madness and guilt—speaking of them as
incurable from generation to generation. He contrasts the end
of the wicked and the end of the righteous; "like sheep the
former are laid in the grave," buried out of sight, forgotten,
unmourned. "Over them the righteous shall have dominion
in the morning." The morning then brings dominion to
the righteous—redemption from the power of the grave.
In this Jesus rejoiced; in this let us rejoice. This joy of the
morning was set before Him; it is the same joy that is set
before us. Dominion in the morning is that to which we look
forward—a share in the first resurrection, of which they who
are partakers live and reign with Christ.

Look again at the forty-sixth Psalm. It is the utterance
of the faith of Israel's faithful ones, in the time of "Jacob's
trouble." The earth is shaken (verse 2, compared with Hag.
2:6; and Heb. 12:26, 27); the sea and the waves roar (verse 3,
comp. with Luke 21:25): but there is a river whose streams
gladden them. God is in the midst of her. Nay, "God helps
her when the morning appeareth" (verse 5, margin), just as
in the morning watch He looked out from the fiery cloud and
troubled the Egyptians. Then the heathen are scattered at
His voice, He sweeps off every enemy, He makes wars to
cease, and sets Himself on high over the nations, as King of
kings, "exalted in the earth." From which we gather that the
morning brings with it deliverance from danger, victory over
enemies, the renewal of the earth, peace to the nations, the
establishment of Messiah's glorious throne. What a morning
of joy must that be, for the church, for Israel, for the whole
earth—resurrection for the church, restoration for Israel,
restitution for the earth!

Look at the 110th Psalm. We see Jesus at Jehovah's right

hand, waiting till His enemies be made His footstool; and then He who said unto Him "Sit," shall say "Arise" (Ps. 82:8). He is yet to have dominion on earth, and to sit upon the throne of His father David. Instead of "a gainsaying people," as He had in the day of His weakness, He is to have "a willing people in the day of His power;" all arrayed in the beauties of holiness; more numerous and resplendent than the dew from the womb of the morning. Willingness, beauty, holiness, brightness, number—these shall mark His people in that morning of joy which His coming shall produce. "The dew (says one) is deposited in greatest plenty about the breaking of the dawn, and refresheth with its numerous drops the leaves and plants and blades of grass on which it resteth; so shall the saints of God, coming forth from their invisible abodes out of the womb of the morning, refresh the world with their benignant influence; and therefore are they likened to the dew, for all nature is so constituted of God, as to bear witness of that day of regeneration which then shall dawn."

Read also "the last words of David" (2 Sam. 23:1–4), in which, as in the seventy-second Psalm, "He that ruleth over men must be just, ruling in the fear of God. And he shall be as the light of the morning, when the sun riseth, even a morning without clouds; as the tender grass springing out of the earth by clear shining after rain." Not till that Just One comes is the morning to dawn, for He is its light; and from His countenance is to break forth that light in which all earth is to rejoice. Then the darkness of the long night shall disappear, and the brief tribulation tasted in the time of absence be forgotten in the abounding blessedness of His everlasting presence.

Let us hear how, in "the Song," the bride refers to this same morning. She rejoices in the Bridegroom's assured love, and her desires or longings are not questionings as to the relationship in which she stands to Him. This is with her a settled thing, for she has tasted that the Lord is gracious. "I am my beloved's, and my beloved is mine." What direction then do her longings take? Her "eyes are towards the hills," over which she expects to behold Him coming like a roe. Thus she pleads with Him not to tarry; "Make haste, my beloved, and be thou like to a roe, or to a young hart upon the mountains of spices" (8:14). Thus also she anticipates the morning of fuller joy, even while enjoying present fellowship; "He feedeth among the lilies until the day break and the shadows flee away" (2:16, 17). And thus the Bridegroom Himself, feeling, if one may so speak, the loneliness of the night, and that it is "not good to be alone," longs, like herself, for day, and resolves to climb the hills, where He may not only be regaled with freshest odors, but may catch the earliest gleam of dawn: "Until the day break, and the shadows flee away, I will get me to the mountain of myrrh, and to the hill of frankincense" (4:6). On that hill let us meet Him in faith, and watch with Him in hope, yet ever remembering, that though this joy which faith gives here is unspeakably comforting, it is not the gladness of the marriage supper, it is not the blessedness of the bridal day. For He Himself, while telling His disciples, "Lo, I am with you always," says also this, "I will not henceforth drink of this fruit of the vine until the day that I shall drink it new with you in my Father's kingdom" (Matt. 26:29).

Thus we see all kinds of joy brought within the circle of this morning. It is a morning of joy, because it is the morning introduced by Him who said, "These things have I spoken unto you, that my joy might remain in you, and that your joy might be full" (John 15:11); by Him "in whose presence there is fullness of joy, and at whose right hand there are pleasures for evermore" (Ps. 16:11). But let us mark the different kinds of joy and the different figures denoting it.

There is the joy of deliverance from overwhelming danger. This was the joy of the Jews when their adversary perished, and Mordecai was exalted; "The Jews had light, and gladness, and joy, and honour, …the Jews had joy and gladness, a feast and a good day" (Esth. 8:16). Such shall be the church's joy in the morning of her great deliverance. There is the joy of escape from captivity and return from exile, such as made Israel feel "like them that dream." Such shall be the church's joy when her long captivity is done. Then shall her mouth be filled with laughter, and her tongue with singing. "They that sow in tears shall reap in joy" (Ps. 126:5). There is the joy of harvest (Isa. 9:3); and such shall be the church's joy. There is the mother's joy when her pangs are over, and the child is born into the world (John 16:20). With such joy shall we rejoice, and our joy no man taketh from us. The joy in reserve for us is manifold and large; it will abide and satisfy; it is the joy of the *morning*—a long glad day before us; no evening with its lengthening shadows, no night with its chills and darkness. "There shall be no night there; and they need no candle, neither light of the sun; for the Lord God giveth them light: and they shall reign for ever and ever" (Rev. 22:5).

The prospect of this morning—this "morning of joy"—nerves and cheers us under all our tribulation. Were this morning an uncertainty, how dark would the night seem; how difficult for us to fight against faintness and despair! But the thought of morning invigorates and braces us. We can set our faces to the storm, for behind it lies the calm. We can bear the parting, for the meeting is not distant. We can afford to weep, for the tear shall soon be wiped away. We can watch the tedious sick bed, for soon "the inhabitant shall not say, I am sick." We can look quietly into the grave of buried love and cherished hope for resurrection shines beyond it. Things may be *against us* here, but they are for us hereafter. The *here* is but an hour; the *hereafter* is a whole eternity.

But for the world—the heedless, pleasure-chasing world, they have no such brightening for their dark hours of sorrow. No morning comes to them. Their sun sets, but rises not again; their life goes down in darkness, without a hope. It is night—night infinite and endless, to them; "the blackness of darkness for ever!" No healing of their wounds, no wiping away of their tears, no binding up of their broken hearts! They reject the infinite sacrifice, they sport away their day of salvation, and their history winds up in judgment and the second death. "If they speak not according to this word" (says the prophet), *"there is no morning for them"* (Isa. 8:20, margin). This *word,* "which by the gospel is preached unto them" (1 Peter 1:25) they slight or scorn, and vengeance overtakes them for rejection! "Therefore," says the same prophet, "shall evil come upon you; *thou shalt not know its morning"* (Isa. 47:11, margin). An evil without a deliverance, a night without a morning, is their portion!

Sad closing of a life-time's weariness! Joy they have never known, though its full cup has often been handed to them by God, and they pressed to drink it! For what is each message, each summons, each warning, but God saying to them, "Come share my love, come taste my joy!" Sorrow they have known, for how could they miss knowing it in such a world! Heavy burdens, keen griefs, sharp stings, bitter memories, hard misgivings, intolerable forebodings, dark self-questionings: "What am I, or what shall I be?" All these, crowding in upon a soul that has no God, pouring into a heart that has no outlet for its sorrows in the bosom of a Savior, are enough to dry up life's springs even when deepest. Yet all these are but the beginning of sorrows! There is a fuller cup yet to be given to them to drink—eternal wormwood! Then the heart would fain break, but cannot. For the sorrow is as eternal as it is infinite. They shall seek for death, but shall not be able to find it; for the second death is the death that never dies.

7

The Victory over Death

The issue of the conflict between the saints and death was decided when the Lord arose. He met the enemy on his own territory, his own battle-field, and overcame. He entered the palace of the king of terrors, and there laid hold of the strong man, shaking his dwelling to its foundations as he came forth, carrying away its gates along with Him, and giving warning of being about to return, in order to complete His conquest by "spoiling his goods," and robbing him of the treasures which he had kept so long—the dust of sleeping saints.

The first act of spoiling the strong man of his goods begins at the resurrection. Of this we have already spoken *generally,* but the subject is so largely dwelt upon in Scripture, that something more special is needed. For it is a hope so fruitful in consolation to us who are still sojourners in a dying world like this, and yet so little prized, that we must not pass it slightly by.

Let us look at it in the aspects in which the apostle spreads it out before us in the fifteenth chapter of his first epistle to the Corinthians.

The vision which he there holds before us is one of glory and joy. It is a *morning* landscape, and contrasts brightly with present night and sorrow. It draws aside the veil that hides from view our much-longed-for heritage, showing us from our prospect-hill the excellence of the land that shall so soon be ours—plains richer than Sharon, valleys more fruitful than Sibmah, mountains goodlier than Carmel or Lebanon. The *then* and the *now*, the *there* and the *here*, are strangely diverse. Here the mortal, there the immortal; here the corruptible, there the incorruptible; here the earthly, there the heavenly; here the dominion of death, there death swallowed up of victory; here the grave devouring its prey, there the spoiler of the grave coming forth in resurrection-power, to claim each particle of holy dust, undoing death's handiwork, spoiling the spoiler, bringing forth in beauty that which had been laid down in vileness, clothing with honor that which had been sown in shame.

"The trumpet shall sound, the dead shall be raised incorruptible, and we shall be changed!" All this "in a moment, in the twinkling of an eye." Other changes are gradual, this sudden. There is the ebbing and the flowing; there is the growing up into manhood, and the growing down into old age; there is the slow opening of spring into summer, and of summer into autumn; but this shall be unlike all these changes. It shall be instantaneous, like the lightning's flash, or the twinkling of an eye. He who spake and it was done, shall speak again, and it shall be done; He who said, "Let there be light," and there was light, shall speak, and light shall come forth out of the grave's thick darkness.

"This corruptible shall put on incorruption"! There will be an entire casting aside of mortality with all its wrappings of corruption, with all its relics of dishonor. Every particle of evil shall be shaken out of us, and "this vile body" transfigured into the likeness of the Lord's own glorious body. We entered this world mortal and corruptible; all our life long we are imbibing mortality and corruption, becoming more and more thoroughly mortal and corruptible; the grave sets its seal to all this, and crumbles us down into common earth. But the trumpet sounds, and all this is gone. Mortality falls off, and all pertaining to it is left behind. No more of dross or disease in our frame. We can then defy sickness, and pain, and death. We can say to our bodies, be pained no more; to our limbs, be weary no more; to our lips, be parched no more; to our eye, be dim no more.

"O death, where is thy sting?" He that hath the power of death is the devil, the old serpent, and he torments us here. Sin gave him his sting, and the law gave sin its strength; but now that sin has been forgiven and the law magnified, the sting is plucked out. The stinging begins with our birth; for life throughout is one unceasing battle with death, until, for a season, death conquers, and we fall beneath his power. But the prey shall be taken from the mighty and his victims rescued for ever. Now sin has passed away, and what has become of death's sting—its sharpness, its pain, its power to kill? It cannot touch the immortal and the incorruptible!

"O grave, where is now thy victory?" A conqueror all along hast thou been, never yet baffled, thy course one perpetual triumph, the ally of death, following in his footsteps; not only smiting down the victim, but devouring it, taking it into thy den, and consuming it bone by bone, till every particle is crumbled into dust, as if to make victory so sure that a retrieval of it would be absolutely impossible. Yet thy victories are over; the tide of battle is turned in the twinkling of an eye. Look at these rising myriads—thou canst hold them no longer: thou thoughtest them thy prey, when they were but given to keep for a little moment. See these holy ones, without one spot, not one stain on which thy sting, O death, can fasten; not a weakness, which might encourage thee again to hope for a second victory! All thy doings of six thousand years undone in a moment! Not a scar remaining from all thy many wounds; not a trace, or disfigurement, or blot—all perfection, eternal beauty! And look at these other holy ones, also glorified! They have not tasted death, nor passed down into the grave. Over them thou hast had no power. Thou hast waged war with them in vain.

They have seen no corruption, and they remain monuments that thou wert not invincible. They have defied the power, and now they are beyond thy reach!

Ah, this is victory! It is not escaping by stealth out of the hands of the enemy, it is conquering him! It is not bribing him to let us go; it is open and triumphant victory—victory which not only routs and disgraces the enemy, but swallows him up—victory achieved in righteousness, and in behalf of these who had once been "lawful captives."

And the victor, who is He? Not we, but our Brother-king. His sword smote the mighty one, and under His shield we have come off conquerors. The wreath is His of victorious battle, not ours; we are the trophies, not the conquerors. He overcame. How? By allowing Himself to be overcome! He plucked the sting from death. How? By allowing it to pierce Himself! He made the grave to let go its hold. How? By going down into its precincts and wrestling with it in the greatness of His strength. He brought round the law which was against us to be upon our side. How? By giving the law all that it sought, so that it could ask no more either of Him or of us.

How complete the victory over us seemed for a while to be, yet how complete the reversal! These enemies are not only conquered, but more than conquered. No trace of their former conquests remains. We not only live, but are made immortal. We not only are rescued from the corruption of the grave, but made incorruptible for ever.

Victory, then, is our watchword. We entered on the conflict at first, assured of final victory by Him who said, "I am the resurrection and the life; he that believeth on me, though he were dead yet shall he live, and whosoever liveth and believeth on me shall never die"; by Him who to all His many promises of spiritual life and blessing added this, "and I will raise him up at the last day." When taking up sword and shield, we were sure of success; we could boast when putting on the harness as he that putteth it off in triumph.

Victory was our watchword during every conflict, even the hardest and the sorest. Victory was our watchword on the bed of death, in the dark valley, when going down for a season into the tomb. Victory is to be our final watchword when re-appearing from the grave, leaving mortality beneath us, and ascending to glory.

"Then shall Jehovah God wipe away tears from off all faces" (Isa. 25:8; 30:19; 35:10; 60:20; Jer. 31:12; Rev. 7:17; 21:4). We shall weep no more. The furrows of past tears are effaced. Tears of anguish, tears of parting, tears of bereavement, tears of adversity, tears of heart-breaking sorrow, these are forgotten. We *cannot* weep again. The fountain of tears is dried up. God our Lord wipes up the tears. It is not *time* that heals the sorrows of the saints, or dries up their tears, it is God; God Himself; God alone. He reserves this for Himself, as if it were His special joy. The world's only refuge in grief is *time,* or pleasure; but the refuge of the saints is God. This is the true healing of the wound; and the assurance to us that tears once wiped away by God cannot flow again.

"The rebuke of his people shall he take away from off all the earth" (Isa. 25:8). As He is to do this for Israel, so also for the church. Rebuke, reproach, persecution, have been the church's lot on earth. The world hated the Master, and they have hated the servant. "The reproach of Christ" (Heb. 11) is a well-known reproach. Shame for His Name is what His saints have been enduring, and shall endure until He comes again. But all this is to be reversed. Soon the world's taunt shall cease. They shall scorn no more; they shall hate no more; they shall revile no more, and no more cast out our names as evil. Honor crowns the saints, and their enemies are put to shame. It is but one day's reviling before men, and then an eternity of glory in the presence of God and of the Lamb. Then the name of saint shall be a name of glory, both in earth and heaven.

Why shrink then from the world's reproach, when it is but a breath at the most, and when we know that it so soon shall cease? Why not rejoice that we are counted worthy to suffer shame for the name of Jesus, when we know that all that afflicts us here is not worthy to be compared with the glory that shall be revealed in us? The morning, and the glory which the morning brings with it, will more than compensate for all. Let us be of good cheer then, and press onward, through evil report as well as through good, having respect unto the recompense of reward.

"Creation shall be delivered from the bondage of corruption into the glorious liberty of the sons of God." That morning which brings resurrection to us brings restitution to creation—deliverance to a groaning earth. The same Lord that brings us out of the tomb, rolls back the curse from off creation, effacing the vestiges of the first Adam's sin, and presenting a fresh memorial of the second Adam's righteousness. Happy world, when Satan is bound, when the curse is obliterated, when the bondage is broken, when the air is purged, when the soil is cleansed, when the grave is emptied, and when the risen saints take the throne of creation to rule in righteousness with the scepter of the righteous King!

Resurrection is our hope; our hope in life, our hope in death. It is a purifying hope. It is a gladdening hope. It comforts us when laying in the grave the clay of those whom we have loved. It cheers us when feeling the weakness of our own frame, and thinking how soon we shall lie down in dust. It refreshes and elevates when we remember how much precious dust earth has received since the day of righteous Abel. How sweet that name—resurrection! It pours life into each vein and vigor into each nerve at the very mention of it!

It is not carnal thus to bend over the clay-cold corpse and long for the time when these very limbs shall move again; when that hand shall clasp ours as of old; when those eyes shall brighten; when those lips shall resume their suspended utterance; when we shall feel the throbbings of that heart again! No, it is scriptural, it is spiritual. Some may call it *sentimental;* but it is our very nature. We cannot feel otherwise, even if we would. We cannot but love the clay. We cannot but be loath to part with it. We cannot but desire its reanimation. The nature that God has given us can be satisfied with nothing less. And with nothing less has God purposed to satisfy it. "Thy brother shall rise again." "Them also which sleep in Jesus will God bring with him."

We feel the weight of that mortality that often makes life a burden; yet we say, "Not that we would be unclothed, but clothed upon, that mortality may be swallowed up of life." We lay within the tomb the desire of our eyes, yet we cling to the remains, and feel as if the earth that struck the coffin were wounding the body on which it falls. At such a moment the thought of opening graves and rising dust is unutterably precious. We shall see that face again. We shall hear that voice again. Not only does the soul that filled that clay still live, but that clay itself shall be revived. Our *risen* friend shall be in very deed—form, look, voice—the friend that we have known and loved. Our risen brother will be all that we knew him here when, hand in hand, we passed through the wilderness together, cheered with the blessed thought that no separation could part us long, and that the grave itself could unlink neither hands nor hearts.

8

The Reunion

The family has been all along a scattered one. Not only has it been scattered along the ages, but it has been dispersed over every land. "Children of the dispersion" might well be the name of its members. They have no continuing city, nay, no city at all that they can call their own; sure of nothing here beyond their bread and raiment; nowhere able to reckon upon a certain dwelling, yet having always the promise of it somewhere.

Besides this scattering, arising from their being thus called out of every kindred and nation, there are others more bitter. There is the scattering which persecution makes, when it drives them from city to city. There is the scattering which adversity makes when happy circles are broken up, and their fragments sent far asunder. There is the scattering which oftentimes jealousy and contention and selfish rivalry produce, even among the saints. There is the scattering which bereavement makes, when strong ties are broken, and warm love spilt like water on the ground; when fellowship is rent asunder, and living sympathies chilled by death, and tears of choking anguish are all the relief of loneliness and sorrow.

As Israel was scattered among the nations, so have the saints been; not indeed like Israel, because of the wrath of God against them, but still scattered everywhere. "The Lord shall scatter thee among all people, from the one end of the earth even unto the other" (Deut. 28:64), were God's words to Israel, and the church feels how truly they suit her condition as a scattered flock.

In primitive times, and often since that, in days of trouble and persecution, it was truly and literally a *scattering,* just as when the autumn wind shakes down and tosses the ripe leaves to and fro. But in our day it is not so much a scattering, as a simple dwelling asunder, by the calling out of every nation the few that make up the little flock. It is a gathering *out,* but not a gathering *together.* It is one family, yet the members know not, see not each other in the flesh. They are drawn by the Father's hand, and according to the Father's purpose, out of kingdoms and families wide asunder. They have no local center, either of interest, or of residence, or of government; no common home, no common meeting-place, save that which faith gives them now in their Head above, or that hope assures them of in the world to come, where they shall come together, face to face, as one household, gathered under one roof, and seated around one table.

This separation and apparent disunion is not natural or congenial. For there is a hidden magnetic virtue which unconsciously and irresistibly draws them towards each other. Separation is the present law of the kingdom, but this only because *election* is the law of the dispensation. There is an affinity among the members which neither time nor distance can destroy. There is a love kindled they know not how, kept alive they know not how, but strong and unquenchable, the love of kin, the love of brotherhood:

> *No distance breaks the tie of blood.*
> *Brothers are brothers evermore.*

And they feel this. Knit by the ties of a strange and unearthly union, they have a conscious feeling of oneness which nothing can shake. Deep hidden in each other's "heart of hearts" they cannot consent to be perpetually asunder, but eagerly anticipate the day of promised union.

But there is another kind of separation which they have
had to endure. Death has torn them from each other. From
Abel downward there has been one long scene of bereavement.
The griefs of parting make up the greatest amount of earthly
suffering among the children of men. And from these griefs
the saints have not been exempted. Bitter have been the
farewells that have been spoken on earth—around the deathbed, or in the prison, or on the sea-shore, or on the home
threshold, or in the city of strangers—the farewells of men
who knew that they should no more meet till the grave gave
up its trust. Death has been the great scatterer, and the tomb
has been the great receiver of the fragments.

Our night of weeping has taken much of its gloom and
sadness from these rendings asunder. The pain of parting, in
the case of the saints, has much to alleviate it, but still the
bitterness is there. We feel that we must separate, and though
it be only for a while, still our hearts bleed with the wound.

But there is *reunion*. And one of the joys of the morning
is this reunion among the saints. During the night they had
been scattered, in the morning they are gathered together. In
the wilderness they have been separated, but in the kingdom
they shall meet. During this age they have been like the drops
of the fitful shower; in the age to come they shall be like the
dew of Hermon, the dew that descended upon the mountains
of Zion, one radiant company, alighting upon the holy hills,
and bringing with them refreshment to a weary earth. Then
shall fully be answered the prayer of the Lord, "That they
all may be one; as thou, Father, art in me, and I in thee, that
they also may be one in us: that the world may believe that
thou hast sent me. And the glory which thou gavest me I have
given them; that they may be one, even as we are one; I in
them, and thou in me, that they may be made perfect in one;
and that the world may know that thou hast sent me, and hast
loved them as thou hast loved me" (John 17:21–23).

"I will smite the Shepherd, and the sheep of the flock

shall be scattered abroad" (Matt. 26:31). Such is our present position—a *smitten* Shepherd and a *scattered* flock! But the day is at hand when "he that scattered shall gather," and there shall be a *glorified* Shepherd and a *gathered* flock; not merely one flock, one fold, and one Shepherd, but one flock gathered into the one fold around the one Shepherd, the scattering ceased, the wandering at an end, the famine exchanged for the green pastures, the danger forgotten, and the devouring lion bound. Then shall fully come to pass the prophecy regarding the issues of the Surety's death, "that he should gather together in one the children of God that were scattered abroad" (John 11:52). Then what is written of Israel shall, in a higher sense, be fulfilled in the church: "Behold, I, even I, will both search my sheep, and seek them out. As a shepherd seeketh out his flock in the day that he is among his sheep that are scattered; so will I seek out my sheep, and will deliver them out of all places where they have been scattered in the cloudy and dark day. I will feed them in a good pasture, and upon the high mountains of Israel shall their fold be. And I will set up one shepherd over them, and he shall feed them, even my servant David; he shall feed them, and he shall be their shepherd." And as the ingathering of Israel is to be a blessing diffusing itself on every side, so is the reunion of the scattered church to be to the world; so that we may use Israel's promise here also: "I will make them and the places round about my hill a blessing; and I will cause the shower to come down in his season; there shall be showers of blessing" (Ezek. 34:11–26).

This reunion is when the Lord returns. When the Head appears, then the members come together. They have been always united, for just as the Godhead was still united to the manhood of Christ, even when His body was in the tomb, so the oneness between the members, both with each other and with their Head, has been always kept unbroken. But when He comes, this union is fully felt, realized, seen, manifested.

"When Christ, who is our life, shall appear, then shall ye also appear with him in glory" (Col. 3:4).

This reunion is at "the resurrection of the just." Then every remaining particle of separation is removed—soul and body meet—both perfect; no trace of this "vile body," or this dust-cleaving soul. The corruptible has gone, and the incorruptible has come. Our reunion shall be in incorruption; hands that shall never grow palsied clasping each other, and renewing broken companionships, eyes that shall never dim gazing on each other with purer love.

This reunion is in the cloud of glory, in which the Lord comes again. When he went up from Olivet, this cloud received him, and fain would his disciples have gone up along with him. But into that glorious pavilion—His tabernacle—shall they yet ascend; there to meet with Him, and to embrace each other, coming together into that mysterious dwelling-place, from the four winds of heaven, "out of every kindred, and nation, and tongue, and people."

This reunion is the marriage-day, and that cloud-curtained pavilion the Bridegroom's chamber. There the bride is now seen as *one*. And there she realizes her own oneness in a way unimagined before. There, too, the marriage-feast is spread, and the bride takes her place of honor at the marriage-table—"glorious within," as well as without—not, like the harlot-bride, decked with purple, and scarlet, and gold, and gems (Rev. 17:4; 18:16); but "arrayed in fine linen, clean and white" (19:8).

It is to this reunion, and to the honors that shall then be given to the whole church at once, that the apostle refers, when he says, that "they (the Old Testament saints, to whom the promises came) without us should not be made perfect" (Heb. 11:39, 40). Thus he intimates that the actual possession of the thing promised has not yet been given. It is deferred until the Lord comes, in order that no age, nor section, nor individuals of the church should be perfectly blest and glorified before the rest; for all must be raised up together, all caught up together, all crowned together, seeing they are one body, one bride. He points to the day of the Lord as the day of our common introduction into the inheritance, the day of our common re-entrance into Eden, the day when, as one vast multitude of all kindreds, we shall enter in through the gates into the city; the day of our common crowning, our common triumph. For it is to be *one* crowning, *one* enthroning, *one* festival, *one* triumph, *one* entrance for the whole church, from the beginning. The members are not crowned alone, nor in fragments, nor in sections; but in one glorious hour they receive their everlasting crowns, and take their seats, side by side, with their Lord, and with each other, in simultaneous gladness, upon the long-expected throne.

The preparations for this union have long been making. They began with us individually, when first the scattered fragments of our souls were brought together by the Holy Ghost, at our conversion. Before that, our "hearts were divided"; and this was our special sin (Hos. 10:2). But then they "were united," at least in some measure, though still calling for the unceasing prayer, "Unite my heart to fear thy name" (Ps. 86:11). It was first the *inner* man that came under the power of sin and was broken into parts; then the *outer* man followed. Both were created whole in every sense of that word, and both have ceased to be whole in any sense of it. When restoration begins, it begins with the reunion of the inner man, and in the resurrection passes on to the outer, bringing together the two restored parts. It was the *individual* that first was subjected to sin, and then the *mass*. So it is the individual that is first restored. And this is the process that is now going on under the almighty, vivifying, uniting energy of the Holy Spirit. But the reunion is not complete till oneness is brought back to the mass, to the body, till all those members that have been singly restored be brought together, and so the body made *whole*.

It is for this we wait until the Lord comes. For as it was the first Adam that broke creation into fragments, so it is the second Adam that is to restore creation in all its parts and regions, and make it one again. The good and the evil then are parted for ever, but the good and the good are brought into perfect oneness—a oneness so complete, so abiding, as more than to compensate for brokenness and separation here.

The soul and the body come together and form one glorified man. The ten thousand members of the church come together and form one glorified church. The scattered stones come together and form one living temple. The bride and the Bridegroom meet. *Here* it has been one Lord, one faith, one baptism; *there* it shall be one body, one bride, one vine, one temple, one family, one city, one kingdom.

The broken fruitfulness, the fitful inconstancy, of the cursed earth shall pass into the unbroken beauty of the new creation. The discord of the troubled elements shall be laid, and harmony return. The warring animals shall lie down in peace.

Then shall heaven and earth come together into one. That which we call distance is annihilated, and the curtain drawn by sin is withdrawn from between the upper and the lower glory, and the fields of a paradise that was never lost are brought into happy neighborhood with the fields of paradise regained; God's purpose developing itself in the oneness of a two-fold glory—the rulers and the ruled, the risen and the unrisen, the celestial and the terrestrial—the glory that is in the heaven above, the glory that is in the earth beneath; for "there are celestial bodies and bodies terrestrial, but the glory of the celestial is one, and the glory of the terrestrial is another."

Such scenes we need to dwell upon, that as our tribulations abound, so also our consolations may abound. Our wounds here are long in healing. Bereavements keep the heart long bleeding. Melancthon, with a tender simplicity so like himself, refers to his feelings when his child was taken from him by death. He wept as he recalled the past. It pierced his soul to remember the time, when once, as he sat weeping, his little one with its little napkin wiped the tears from his cheeks.

Recollections like these haunt us through life, ever and anon newly brought up by passing scenes. Some summer morning's sun recalls, with stinging freshness, the hour when that same sun streamed in through our window upon a dying infant's cradle, as if to bring out all the beauty of a parting smile, and engrave it upon our hearts for ever. Or is it a funeral scene that comes up to memory—a funeral scene that had but a few days before been a bridal one—and never on earth can we forget the outburst of our grief, when we saw the bridal flowers laid upon a new-made tomb. Or some wintry noon recalls the time and the scene when we laid a parent's dust within its resting-place, and left it to sleep in winter's grave of snows. These memories haunt us, pierce us, and make us feel what a desolate place this is, and what an infinitely desirable thing it would be to meet these lost ones again, where the meeting shall be eternal.

Hence the tidings of this reunion in the many mansions are like home-greetings. They relieve the smitten heart. They bid us be of good cheer, for the separation is but brief, and the meeting to which we look forward will be the happiest ever enjoyed. The time of sorrowful recollections will soon pass, and no remembrance remain but that which will make our joy to overflow.

Every thing connected with this reunion is fitted to enhance its blessedness. To meet again any where, or any how, or at any time would be blessed; how much more at such a time, in such circumstances, and in such a home! The dark past lies behind us like a prison from which we have come forth, or like a wreck from which we have escaped in safety and landed in a quiet haven. We meet where separation is an impossibility, where distance no more tries fidelity, or pains the spirit, or mars the joy of loving. We meet in a kingdom. We meet at a marriage-table. We meet in the "prepared city," the New Jerusalem. We meet under the shadow of the tree of life, and on the banks of the river of life. We meet to keep festival and sing the songs of triumph. It was blessed to meet here for a day; how much more to meet in the kingdom for ever! It was blessed to meet, even with parting full in view; how much more so when no such cloud overhangs our future! It was blessed to meet in the wilderness and the land of graves; how much more in paradise, and in the land where death enters not! It was blessed to meet "in the night," though chill and dark; how much more in the morning, when light has risen, and the troubled sky is cleared, and joy is spreading itself around us like a new atmosphere, from which every element of sorrow has disappeared.

9

The Presence of the Lord

To love in absence, though with the knowledge of being beloved, and with the certainty of meeting ere long, is but a mingled joy. It contents us in the room of something better and more blessed, but it lacks that which true love longs for, the presence of the beloved one. That presence fills up the joy and turns every shadow into brightness.

Especially when this time of absence is a time of weakness and suffering, and endurance of wrong; when dangers come thickly around, and enemies spare not, and advantage is taken by the strong to vex or injure the defenceless. Then love in absence, though felt to be a sure consolation, is found to be insufficient, and the heart cheers itself with the thought that the interval of loneliness is brief, and that the days of separation are fast running out.

It is with such feelings that we look forward to our meeting with Him "whom having not seen we love," and anticipate the joy of being for ever "with the Lord." That day of meeting has in it enough of gladness to make up for all the past. And then it is eternal. It is not meeting today, and parting to-morrow; it is meeting once and forever. To see Him face to face, even for a day, how blessed! To be "with Him" for a lifetime, or an age, even though with intervals of absence between, how gladdening! But to be with Him for ever—or *always,* as it stands in the original—this surely is the very filling up of all our joy.

Has not the Lord, however, been always with us? Has He not said, "Lo, I am with you alway, even unto the end of the world"? Yes. Nor ought the church to undervalue this nearness, this fellowship. It is no shadow or fancy; it is reality. It is that same reality to which the Lord referred when He said, "He that loveth me shall be loved of my Father; and I will love him, and will manifest myself to him" (John 14:21); or, as the old versions have it, "will show mine own self to him." For when Jude put the question, "Lord, how is it that thou wilt manifest thyself to us and not unto the world?" that is, "How shall it be that the world shall not see Thee, and yet we who are living in the world shall see Thee? How is it that we shall have Thy presence, and yet the world have it not?" "Jesus answered and said unto him, If a man love me he will keep my words; and my Father will love him, and we will come unto him, and make our abode with him."

So that thus we have had the Lord always with us, nay, making His abode with us. It was when first we gave credit to the divine testimony concerning the free love of God, in the gift of His Son, that we drew nigh to Him and He to us. It was then that He came in unto us, and took up His abode with us. It was when we heard His voice and opened the door, that He came in to sup with us. And it is this conscious presence—this presence which faith realizes—that cheers us amid tribulation here. In the furnace we have one like the Son of man to keep us company, and to prevent the flame from kindling upon us.

But this is, after all, incomplete. It is the enjoyment of as much fellowship as can be tasted in absence, but it is no more. Nor is it intended to supersede something nearer and more complete, far less to make us content with absence. Nay, its tendency is to make us less and less satisfied with absence. It gives us such a relish for intercourse, that we long for communion more unhindered—eye to eye and face to face. This closer intercourse, this actual vision, this bodily nearness, we are yet to enjoy. The hope given us is to be "with the Lord"—with him in a way such as we have never been.

Let no one despise this nearness, nor speak evil of it, as if it were material and carnal. Many speak as if their bodies were a curse, as if matter were some piece of mis-creation to which we had unnaturally and unhappily been fastened. And others tell us that actual intercourse, such as we refer to, the intercourse of vision and voice, is a poor thing, not to be named beside the other, which is, as they conceive, the deeper and the truer.

But is it so? Is matter so despicable? Are our bodies such hindrances to true fellowship? Is the eye nothing, the ear nothing, the smile nothing, the voice nothing, the embrace nothing, the clasping of the hand nothing? Is personal communion a hindrance to earthly friendships? Can the friend enjoy the friend as well afar off as near? Is it no matter to the wife though her husband be unseen and distant? Granting that we can still love and receive love in return, is distance no barrier, does absence make no blank? Do we slight bodily presence, visible intercourse, as worthless, almost undesirable? Is not the reverse one of the most deep-seated feelings of our nature? And is it not to this deep-seated feeling that the incarnation appeals? Is that incarnation useless, save as furnishing a victim for the altar, and providing blood for the cleansing of the worshipper? No. The incarnation brings God nigh to us in a way such as could not have been done by any other means. He became bone of our bone and flesh of our flesh, that we might have a being like ourselves to commune with, to love, to lean upon.

In that day when we shall be "with the Lord," we shall know to the full the design of God in the incarnation of His Son, and taste the blessedness of seeing Him as He is.

The time of this meeting is His coming; not till then.

Before that there is distance and imperfection. I know that in the disembodied state there will be greater nearness and fuller enjoyment than now. And this the apostle longed for when he had the "desire to depart and be with Christ, which is far better." Even before the resurrection there is a "being with Christ," more satisfying than what we enjoy here; a "being with Christ" which is truly "far better." Nor would I disparage this blessedness. But still this is not to be compared with resurrection-nearness, and resurrection-fellowship, when, in a way up till that time unknown, we shall be introduced into the very presence of the King, all distance annihilated, all fellowship completed, all joy consummated, all coldness done away, all shadows dissipated, and "so we shall ever be with the Lord."

But, for the better understanding of this subject, let us look to the way in which the apostle handles it in administering comfort to the Thessalonian church, some of whom had been giving way to immoderate grief for the dead.

The grief of the heathen was immoderate, and their expressions of it equally so. No wonder. Their hearts beat with as firm a pulse as ours, and natural affection was as strong with them as with us. The husband mourned the wife, the wife the husband; the parent mourned the child, the child the parent; friends wept over the grave of friends. The breaking of these ties was bitter; and the special sting was, that they had no hope of reunion. Death to them was a parting for ever; not as when one parts in the morning to meet at even, or as when one parts this year to meet a few years hence. It was a hopeless separation. At the best it was a vague uncertainty, to which deep grief gives no heed; more commonly it was despair. Their sorrow was desperate, their wound incurable.

The Thessalonian saints were sorrowing as those that had no hope, as if they had buried their beloved brethren in an eternal tomb. For this the apostle reproves them. He points out the hope—a sure hope, a blessed hope, a hope fitted to bring true comfort. "Them that sleep in Jesus will God bring with him." They are not lost; they have only been laid to sleep by Jesus, and He will awake them when He returns, and bring them up out of their tombs. Their departure cannot be called dying; it is only sleeping. It has nothing of the despair of death about it. Death has lost its sting; the shroud its gloom; the grave its terrors. It is an end of pain; it is a ceasing from toil. "Blessed are the dead that die in the Lord, for they rest from their labors."

But the apostle looks beyond the resting-place. "Thy brother shall rise again." God Himself will uncover their tomb and call them up, at the return of Him who is the resurrection and the life. And this, says he, "we say unto you by the word of the Lord." He gives this consolation to them as a certainty; having in it nothing vague or doubtful; a certainty proclaimed by himself and resting on the Lord's own words to His disciples ere He left the earth, regarding His advent, and the gathering of His elect to Him.

The Lord is to come! This is the certainty. The Lord is to come! And in that coming are wrapped up all the hopes of His saints.

Of these saints there will be two classes when He comes: (1). *Those that are alive and remain;* the last generation of the church. For, says the apostle elsewhere, "We shall not all sleep, but we shall all be changed" (1 Cor. 15:51). (2). *Those that have fallen asleep;* these forming the larger number, doubtless; for the sleeping ones of all ages shall be there. It might be supposed that the living ones would have the advantage, as being alive when the Lord arrives. But, no, it is not so. They may have some advantages. They never taste death. They are like Enoch and Elijah. They know not the grave. They see no corruption. In their case soul and body are never separated. They do not meet the king of terrors, nor fall under his power.

These are privileges; and yet it might be said, on the other hand, that these saints do not taste the gladness of resurrection; that they are not conformed to their Lord in this, that He died and rose. Still the end in both cases is the same—the one shall have no advantage, no pre-eminence over the other. Both are "presented faultless before the presence of his glory with exceeding joy"; both *equally faultless,* though each has undergone a different process for the accomplishing of this. Thus, the one being changed and the other raised, they are formed into one company, marshaled into one mighty army, and then caught up into the clouds to meet the Lord in the air.

The particulars of this coming, in so far as the apostle gives them, let us briefly look into. "The Lord himself shall descend from heaven." The same Jesus that ascended; He who loved us and washed us from our sins in His own blood; He—His own self—shall come—come in like manner as He was seen go into heaven. "With a shout." This is the shout of a monarch's retinue, the shout of a great army. Just as God is said to have gone up with shouts, so is He to return; return with the shout of the conqueror, the shout of triumph. "The voice of the archangel." A solitary voice is then heard making some mighty announcement, such as that of the angel standing upon sea and earth, and proclaiming that there should be time no longer (Rev. 10:6); or of that other angel, with whose glory the earth was lightened, crying with a loud voice, Babylon is fallen (Rev. 18:2); or of that other angel, who cried with a loud voice to all the fowls of heaven, "Come, gather yourselves unto the supper of the great God" (Rev. 19:17). "The trump of God." It is elsewhere called "the last trump" (1 Cor. 15:52). It is God's own trumpet, the trumpet that awakes the dead; not a voice merely—as if that were too feeble for such a purpose, nor a common trumpet, but the trump of God, one that can pierce the grave and awake the dead.

These are the steps and the accompaniments of the

advent. There is first the shout of the angelic host, as the Redeemer leaves His seat above to take possession of His kingdom here. This shout is continued as He descends. Then, as He approaches nearer, the multitude of the heavenly host is silent, and a solitary voice is heard, the voice of the archangel uttering God's message; then comes the trumpet that calls forth the sleeping just. They obey the call. They arise. No holy dust remains behind. They put on immortality. Then, joined by the transfigured and glorified living, they hasten upwards to the embrace of their beloved Lord.

It is into "the clouds," or "cloud," that they are caught up; that cloud, or clouds, which in all likelihood rested above Eden, making it the place of "the presence of the Lord" (Gen. 3:8; 4:14, 16); which appeared to Moses at the bush; which led Israel over the Red Sea and through the desert; which covered Sinai; which dwelt in the tabernacle and in the temple; which Isaiah saw; which Ezekiel described; which shone down upon the Son of God at His baptism and trans- figuration; which received Him out of sight at His ascension; which Stephen saw when breathing out his soul; which smote Saul to the ground on his way to Damascus; which last of all, appeared to John in Patmos; and which we know shall yet re-appear in the latter day. Into this cloud of the divine presence, this symbol of the excellent glory, Jehovah's tent or dwelling-place, the ark of our safety against the flood of fire, shall the saints be caught up when the Lord appears, and the voice is heard from heaven, "Awake and *sing,* ye that dwell in dust;" and as it was said in Israel, "the song of the Lord be- gan with trumpets" (2 Chron. 29:27), even so with the trump of God shall our resurrection-song begin.

Thus with *songs* shall we go up on high; our songs in the night being exchanged for the songs of the morning. They shall be "songs of deliverance," with which we shall then be "compassed about" in that day when we get up into our "hiding-place" to be "preserved from trouble" (Ps. 32:7); when we "enter into our chambers" and "shut our doors about us," until "the indignation be overpast" (Isa. 26:20). No longer in a strange land or by the rivers of Babylon shall we sing our songs; no longer in "the house of our pilgrimage" or in the wilderness shall we make melody; but in the King's own presence, in the great congregation, in the New Jerusalem which cometh down out of heaven from God. Then "standing upon the sea of glass," and beholding the "judgments of God made manifest" (Rev. 15:2–4), as Israel did when Pharaoh and his chariots sank like lead in the mighty waters, we sing the song of Moses and the song of the Lamb.

Thus "caught up" into the cloud, we *meet* the Lord "in the air," as those do who go forth to meet a friend already on his way to them (Acts 28:15); we meet Him in order that, being there acquitted, acknowledged, and confessed by Him before His Father and before the angels, we may form His retinue, and come with Him to execute vengeance, to judge the world, to share His triumphs, to reign with Him in His glorious kingdom (Zech. 14:5; 1 Thess. 3:13; Jude 14; Rev. 2:26; 3:21).

Thus "meeting the Lord," we are to be "ever with him." He with us and we with Him for ever. "*So* shall we ever be with the Lord;" that is, "*as* we then shall meet, *so* we shall never part;" as is our meeting, so is our eternal communion, our continuance in the presence of His glory. We shall see Him face to face, and His name shall be in our foreheads. Sitting upon the same throne, dwelling under the same roof, hearing His voice, having free access to Him at all times, doing His will, going forth on His errands—this shall be the joy of our eternity. No distance; that is annihilated. No estrangement; that is among the things that are absolutely impossible. No cloud between; that is swept away and cannot re-appear. No coldness; for love is always full. No interruption; for who can come between the Bridegroom and the bride? No change; for He makes us like Himself, without variableness. No parting;

for we have reached our home to go out no more. No end; for the duration of our fellowship is the life of the Ancient of days, of Him who is "from everlasting to everlasting."

"With the Lord!" It would be much to be with Enoch, or with Abraham, or with Moses, or with Elijah, or with Paul; much to share their fellowship, to have converse with them on the things of God and the story of their own wondrous lives; how much more to be "with the Lord!" To be like Peter at His side, like Mary at His feet, like John in His bosom. To have met Him in the streets of Jerusalem, or by the sea of Galilee, or at Jacob's well; to have heard Him name your name, and salute you, as He passed, with the wish of "peace;" to have dwelt in the next house to His at Nazareth, to have been the guest at the table of Lazarus when He was there, to have slept under that roof, it might be in the apartment next the Lord of glory! How much should we have valued privileges such as these, treasuring them in memory, like gold! Nay, even to hear the tidings of His love, to have a message from Him, to be told that He was gracious to us and kept us in mind, to be anywhere beyond the reach of sin and pain, how much! Oh, what then must it be to be "with the Lord"—with Him in His glory; "with him," as the friend is with the friend; "with him," as the bride is with the bridegroom; saying without fear or check, "Let him kiss me with the kisses of his mouth, for thy love is better than wine;" and hearing Him say in return, "Thou art all fair, my love; there is no spot in thee. Come with me from Lebanon, my spouse, with me from Lebanon: look from the top of Amana, from the top of Shenir and Hermon.... Thou hast ravished my heart, my sister, my spouse; thou hast ravished my heart with one of thine eyes, with one turn of thy neck. How fair is thy love, my sister, my spouse! How much better is thy love than wine!" (Song 4:7–10).

"Ever with the Lord!" This soothes all sorrow and sums up all joy. If even here we can say so gladly and so surely,

"I am persuaded that neither death, nor life, nor angels, nor principalities, nor powers, nor things present, nor things to come, nor height, nor depth, nor any other creature, shall be able to separate us from the love of God which is in Christ Jesus or Lord," how much more gladly and surely shall we be able to say it then!

Forever to behold Him shine,
Forevermore to call Him mine!

This is what we look for; this is our watchword and our song even in the day of absence and sorrow; and it is this that makes the expected morning so truly a morning of joy. "As for me, I will behold thy face in righteousness; I shall be satisfied, when I awake, with thy likeness" (Ps. 17:15).

10

The Kingdom

That to which the "much tribulation" leads us, is a kingdom (Acts 14:22). It is to this that it ministers an "abundant entrance" (2 Peter 1:11), an entrance in itself not joyous indeed, but grievous, yet in its issues glorious.

Hitherto it has been *midnight and the wilderness;* ere long it shall be morning and the kingdom. For it is "in the morning" that the righteous are to "have dominion" (Ps. 49:14). Just as the night has been the time of down-treading, and "wearing out," so the morning is the time of having dominion, the time of "bringing judgment to light" (Zeph. 3:5). When "the Just One shall rule over men," he shall be "as the light of the morning when the sun riseth, a morning without clouds" (2 Sam. 23:3, 4). The time when "the Lord shall help," is when "the morning appeareth" (Ps. 46:5, margin); at evening-tide there is trouble, but "before the morning he is not" (Isa. 17:14). The reign of Antichrist is over, and the reign of Christ begins. The kingdom of the unrighteous is broken to pieces, and the kingdom of the righteous rises in its stead. Lucifer, the mock "light-bringer," the false "son of the morning," vanishes from the heavens, and "the true light," the "bright and morning-star," takes His place in the firmament, unclouded and unsetting in His glory. "The kingdom and dominion, and the greatness of the kingdom under the whole heaven, is given to the people of the saints of the Most High" (Dan. 7:27). The church's weary burden is no longer "How long, O Lord," but "The Lord reigneth, let the earth rejoice!" (Ps. 47:1). Her prayer "thy kingdom come," is exchanged for the thanksgiving of the "great voices in heaven," "The kingdoms of this world are become the kingdoms of our Lord, and of his Christ;" "We give thee thanks, O Lord God Almighty, which art, and wast, and art to come, because thou hast taken to thee thy great power, and hast reigned;" "Alleluia, for the Lord God Omnipotent reigneth" (Rev. 11:15; 19:6).

That to which we are hastening on is not merely an inheritance, but a *royal* inheritance—a kingdom. That for which we suffer is a crown. "If we suffer, we shall also reign with him." As we have been truly fellow-sufferers, we shall be as truly fellow-reigners. The suffering has been real, so shall the reigning be. This is "the recompense of reward" to which we have respect when we "choose rather to suffer affliction with the people of God, than to enjoy the pleasures of sin for a season" (Heb. 11:25). This is "the better and the enduring substance," for which we are willing to "endure the great fight of afflictions" (Heb. 10:32, 34). This is the summing up of earth's toil and grief, the issue of a life-time's conflict with weariness, and wrong, and sin.

To think of trial as a preparation for the kingdom is much; but to look at it as an *entrance* into it is more. At the end of time's dark avenue stands the mansion-house, the palace! At the edge of our desert-track lies the kingdom! The avenue may be rugged under foot, thorny on every side, and gloomy over head; the wilderness may be "waste and howling;" yet they are passages—entrances; they are not interminable, and their end is gladness. They usher us into a state which will, in a moment, efface the bitter past, so that it "shall not once be remembered nor come into mind." Thus, though in one aspect tribulation seems a path or gateway fenced with the brier, and hard to fight through; yet in another it is the conqueror's triumphal arch under which we pass into the kingdom; so that while passing through we can sing the song of Him who long ago went this way before us: "I reckon that the sufferings of this present time are not worthy to be compared with the glory that shall be revealed in us" (Rom. 8:18).

The thought of the kingdom cheers us, and the stray gleams of it which faith gives us are like the lattice-lights of a loved dwelling, sparkling through the thicket, to the weary eye of a benighted wanderer. Yes, we are heirs of nothing less than a kingdom, however unlike such we may seem at present, and however ambitious it may be reckoned to claim so much, and to aspire so high. Robes of royalty shall soon cover all our unseemliness; and beneath the glory of a throne we shall bury all our poverty, and shame, and grief.

But this is not all. The varied excellences of that kingdom, as made known to us by prophets and apostles, are such as specially to meet our case, and contrast with our present condition. This fitness, this contrast, makes the thoughts of the kingdom doubly precious and consoling.

1. *It is the kingdom of God (1 Cor. 6:9).* Man's kingdoms have passed away—those kingdoms under which the saints of God have been trodden down. And now all that is *man's* is gone, and nothing remains but what is *God's*! The glory of the kingdom is this, that it is altogether God's. It must, then, be perfect and blessed, wholly unlike any thing that these eyes of ours have seen. If it were but a reformation of human kingdoms, if it were a mere change of dynasty, the prospect of it would be but doubtful comfort; but it is an entire passing away of the old, and a making all things new. It is the return of God to His own world; and oh, what will not that return effect for us! His re-enthronement is what we desire; for it is this alone that gives us the assurance of perpetuity and stability, against which no enemy shall prevail. It was to that re-enthronement

that Jesus looked forward when about to ascend the cross, and of which He spoke twice over at the paschal-table (Luke 22:16, 18); as if this were "the joy set before him," because of which He "endured the cross. despising the shame" (Heb. 12:2). It is that re-enthronement that we also anticipate as the day of our triumph, for then shall we "shine as the sun in the kingdom of our Father" (Matt. 13:43).

2. *It is the kingdom of Christ (Col. 1:13).* This assures that we shall feel at home there. It is no stranger who is to seat us on the throne beside Him; but our nearest of kin, the Man who died for us. It is the pierced hands that wield the scepter. This meets our case. For we are strangers here, specially feeling not at home in the courts and palaces of earth. But then it shall be otherwise. Here we are as men standing outside the kingdoms of the world. They belong to the "prince of this world," but not to Christ, and therefore not to us. They greet us with no friendly welcome. They have no honors for us. They make us stand without. They are to us what Pilate, and Herod, and Annas were to Jesus; they bid us be wronged and smitten, or, at least, look on while we endure "tribulation, distress, persecution, famine, nakedness, peril, sword." Much of the church's tribulation has arisen from the kingdoms of this world *not* being Christ's. But in the age to come, it is Christ that is to reign, all things being put in subjection to Him. He who is to reign knows what it is to be hated by the world, and knows, therefore, how to make up to us, in His kingdom, for all the hatred wherewith we have been hated, and for all the sorrow which has bowed us down while here. And such is obviously the point of Christ's declaration to His disciples (Luke 22:28–30). For having said to them, "Ye are they which have continued with me in my temptations," He adds, "and I appoint unto you a kingdom, as my Father hath appointed unto me; that ye may eat and drink at my table in my kingdom, and sit on thrones, judging the twelve tribes

of Israel"; thus linking together present suffering for Christ and future reigning with Christ—present continuance with Him in trial, and future association with Him in His own kingdom, when He returns to receive the crown.

3. *It is a kingdom not of this world (John 18:36).* The words "not of this world" are, literally, "not out of, or not taken out of, this world;" just as when Christ says, "Ye are of this world, I am not of this world" (John 8:23). This world is wholly evil, and under the dominion of the evil one. Its territory is under a curse. It is called "this present evil world" (Gal. 1:4). It lieth in wickedness (1 John 5:19). Its kingdoms are compared to hideous beasts of prey (Dan. 7), Satan and his hosts, the rulers of the darkness of this world (Eph. 6:12). Thus everything pertaining to it is unholy. Now, the kingdom to come is not fashioned out of its materials, so as to retain any thing of its likeness. Between the kingdoms of this world and the kingdom of the world to come, there is no congeniality or resemblance. Of "this world" it is said, that it rejects the Spirit, nay, it cannot receive Him (John 14:17); but that world is to be full of the Spirit, for "the Spirit is to be poured from on high, and the wilderness is to become a fruitful field" (Isa. 32:15). Of this world Satan is king; of that world Christ is King. This world knows not God, neither the Father nor the Son; but in that world "all shall know him, from the least unto the greatest." In this world all is darkness; in that world all is light. This world is to be fought against and overcome; that world is to be loved and enjoyed. Thus the kingdom of which we are the heirs, is as unlike this world as Eden was unlike the wilderness. And it is this that makes it so desirable. Had it retained any fragments of this world's evil, had it been a mere re-construction of its carnal fabric; had it taken up into itself any of its corrupt qualities, then our comfort were but poor in anticipating its arrival, and counting on the exchange. But it is not of this world, and

this is our joy. We have had enough of this world to make us long for its passing away; and to welcome a kingdom in which no taint or trace of it shall be found.

4. *It is a righteous kingdom.* "The kingdom of God is not meat and drink," that is, not a carnal kingdom, made up of outward observances and sensual dainties, but "*righteousness,* and peace, and joy in the Holy Ghost;" that is, a righteous, peaceful, joyful kingdom, dwelt in and pervaded by the Holy Spirit, so that all belonging to it must be like itself (Rom. 14:17). It is a kingdom whose territory is the "new earth, wherein dwelleth *righteousness*" (2 Peter 3:13). The "unrighteous shall not inherit it" (1 Cor. 6:9); but the *saints* alone shall possess it (Dan. 7:18). The "sceptre of this kingdom is a *righteous* sceptre" (Ps. 45:6). He who wields it is the *righteous* King (Isa. 32:1); "and in his days shall the righteous flourish" (Ps. 72:7). It is a "crown of *righteousness,*" that is laid up for us (2 Tim. 4:8). And then shall "the work of *righteousness* be peace, and the effect of *righteousness* quietness and assurance for ever" (Isa. 32:17). The righteousness of this kingdom makes it unspeakably attractive to those who have been wearied out with the unrighteousness of an unrighteous world. The thought that "the morning" is to bring in that righteous kingdom, comforts us amid the clouds and thick darkness of this night of weeping.

5. *It is a kingdom of peace.* War has by that time run its course; its spears are broken and turned to ploughshares; strife and hatred have fled. The storm has become a calm, and the vexed sea is still. Holy tranquility breathes over earth. "The mountains bring *peace* to the people, and the little hills, by righteousness; there shall be abundance of *peace* so long as the moon endureth (Ps. 72:3–7). "Upon David, and upon his seed, and upon his house, and upon his throne, there shall be *peace for ever* from the Lord" (1 Kings 2:33). Far more truly

than in the days of Solomon there shall be "peace on all sides round about" (1 Kings 4:24); yea, the Lord God will give *rest* on every side, so that there shall be "neither adversary nor evil occurrent" (1 Kings 5:4). Everywhere shall be inscribed the motto upon Gideon's altar, "Jehovah-Shalom" (Judg. 6:24, margin). "The beasts of the field shall be at peace with us" (Job 5:23); for "the wolf shall dwell with the lamb, and the leopard shall lie down with the kid, and the calf and the young lion and the fatling together, and a little child shall lead them; and the cow and the bear shall feed, their young ones shall lie down together. They shall not hurt nor destroy in all my holy mountain" (Isa. 11:6). The groans of creation shall then be over, and its deliverance accomplished. All shall be peace; for the great peace-maker is come. His name is King of Salem, that is, King of peace (Heb. 7:2). He is called "the Prince of Peace," and "of the increase of his government and *peace* there shall be no end" (Isa. 9:6, 7).

With what longing hearts do we desire the arrival of that kingdom, so unlike what this troubled earth has yet known from the beginning hitherto. Each new sorrow stirs the longing. Each new conflict makes us glad at the thought that there is such a kingdom in reserve. Were it not for this, how we should "fret because of evildoers"; and how soon should our patience give way! But with our eye upon this kingdom of peace, we can "glory in tribulation," we can drink the bitterest cup, we can face the thickest storm, we can endure the rudest clamor; and when the world's uproar waxes loudest we can "lift up our heads, knowing that our redemption draweth nigh."

6. *It is a kingdom that cannot be moved* (Heb. 12:28). All other kingdoms have not only been moved, but shaken to pieces. Great Babylon, "the glory of kingdoms," has been a sand-wreath, raised by one tide, and leveled by the next. So have all others been, greater or lesser. One by one they have been

overthrown and crushed, or they have crumbled down and become like the chaff of the summer threshing-floor. But the kingdom that we look for is "the everlasting kingdom of our Lord and Saviour Jesus Christ" (2 Peter 1:11). It abides for ever. Neither force nor age can affect it. It rises out of the ruins of earth's present empires, though unlike them all. The things that can decay or molder are "shaken," in order that they may be *shaken off*, and that those things that cannot be shaken may remain. And thus there comes forth the immovable kingdom, the kingdom into which sin comes not; in which change has no place; into which the curse eats not; of which wisdom and holiness are the strong pillars; where misrule is unknown; where order triumphs; and of which the glory never dims. It is joy to us in such a world of instability and convulsion, to think of such a kingdom. Driven to and fro with the changes of the kingdoms we inhabit here; wearied with the falling and the rising, the casting down and the building up, we long for a kingdom that shall give us rest, a kingdom that cannot be moved. From this uncertainty and fickleness, how many of our griefs have come! For what is there so saddening, so sickening, as the thought that every inch of ground beneath us is shifting, that every prop on which we lean is breaking, that every twig to which we cling is snapping? As we draw our curtains around us, we know not what change, what loss, what sorrow shall greet us on the morrow. Or though going forth light-hearted and unburdened in the morning, we tremble to think what clouds may have gathered over our dwelling ere the evening has fallen. Such is the perishableness, the changeableness of earth and its kingdoms! What joy to look beyond them all, and see through their shadows the everlasting kingdom! Nay, to be assured that this kingdom is at hand, and that ere long He "who is without variableness or shadow of turning," shall bid us welcome to its unchanging rest; and He who is "the same yesterday, today and for ever," shall seat us upon the eternal throne.

"Heaven," says an old writer, "is a company of noble venturers for Christ"; and we may add, of "noble sufferers too." Of such is the kingdom of heaven! It is in that kingdom that we shall rest from our labors, and find the end of all our sufferings. We shall find that we have not ventured too much, nor labored too much, nor suffered too much. The glory of the kingdom will make up for all.

"Fear not, little flock, it is your Father's good pleasure to give you the kingdom." Along with "the King of glory," we shall take our place upon the throne, in that day when, after "raising the poor out of the dust, He shall set them among princes, and make them to inherit the throne of glory"; when the wicked shall be silent in darkness and the adversaries of the Lord shall be broken in pieces"; when "the Lord shall judge the ends of the earth, giving strength unto his king, and exalting the horn of his anointed" (1 Sam. 2:8–10).

"*Thy* kingdom come"! This is the burden of our cries. Weary of man's rule, we long for God's. Sick at heart with this world's scenes of evil—man spoiling man; man enslaving man; man wounding man; man defrauding man; man treading upon man—we long for the setting up of the righteous throne. Oh, what a world will this be, when man's *will* as well as man's *rule* shall be exchanged for Christ's rule and will; when God's "will shall be done on earth even as it is done in heaven"!

It is our joy to think that this kingdom is near; and that there are no centuries of sin and wrong still in reserve either for the church or for the earth. Its *nearness* is our consolation. The hope that it will come cheers us; but the thought *that it is coming soon* cheers us more. For both faith and hope are fed by the thought of nearness. We do not fret at delay, nor grow faint and disconsolate. Yet in some respects our feelings are not unlike those thus described by one of other days,

So tedious is this day,
As is the night before some festival
To an impatient child that hath new robes,
And may not wear them.

Our bridal robes are ready, and we long to put them on. Our priestly royal raiment is also ready, and we desire to exchange for it these weeds of poverty, and shame, and widowhood. Yet "in patience we possess our souls."

We are on the daily out-look for a kingdom, lifting up our heads knowing that our redemption draweth nigh. It will not tarry. The signs of its approach are multiplying. The shadows are still passing and repassing along the grey cliffs, but their increasing rapidity of movement shows a momentous change at hand. Kingdoms are still rising as well as falling, but the deep force of the vibrations—the brevity as well as the abruptness of oscillation—betoken a crisis. At this crisis the world's movements are brought to a stand. Then, touched by a divine hand, they recommence. A better order of rule begins. Satan has been bound (Rev. 20:1–3). "The oppressor has ceased" (Isa. 14:4). He who "smote the people in wrath" is smitten (Isa. 14:6). The misgoverned world rejoices. "The whole earth is at rest and is quiet; they that dwell in it break forth into singing" (Isa. 14:7). The anointed King has appeared. The great kingdom has come!

11

The Grace

Our fountain-head of blessing here is grace. It was to this grace or free love of God that we came when first the consciousness of want and sin awoke within us. This grace of God we found to be large enough for us, and altogether suitable; so that while we felt ourselves unfit objects for anything else, we were just the more, on that account, fit objects for grace. Either for wrath or for grace we were fit, but for nothing else—for nothing between. We shrank from the wrath, and we took refuge in the grace. Between the one and the other, the blood of the accepted sacrifice has made a way, "a way of holiness"; we saw that way, we saw it to be free and unchallenged, we fled along that way, and soon found ourselves beyond the reach of wrath, under the broad covering of grace, nay, under the very wing of the gracious One, of Him who is "full of grace and truth."

It was the knowledge of this grace that rooted up our doubts, that quieted our fears, and made us blush for our unbelief and suspicious mistrust. It is the knowledge of this grace that still keeps our souls in peace, in spite of weakness, and sin, and conflict. Being permitted to draw upon it without limit and without restriction, we feel that no circumstances can arise, in which we shall not be at liberty to use it, nay, in which it is not our chief sin to stand aloof from it, as if it had become less wide and free. With all this large grace placed at our disposal, to draw upon continually, what folly to be afraid of enemies, and evils, and days of trouble! For thus saith the prophet, "Blessed is the man that trusteth in the Lord, and whose hope the Lord is. For he shall be as a tree planted by the waters, and that spreadeth out her roots by the river, and shall not see when heat cometh, but her leaf shall be green; and shall not be careful in the year of drought, neither shall cease from yielding fruit" (Jer. 17:7, 8).

It is in this grace that we "continue" (Acts 13:43). It is in this grace that we "stand" (Rom. 5:2). It is in this grace that we are to "be strong" (2 Tim. 2:1). It is this grace that we are to "hold fast" (Heb. 12:28, margin). It is this grace that is "sufficient for us" (2 Cor. 12:9). It is this grace that we desire for others, saying, "The grace of our Lord Jesus Christ be with you" (Eph. 6:24). All is grace, from the beginning to the end, unmingled grace, in which no respect is had to aught of good done, felt, thought, spoken by us. So that the history of our life is wrapped up in these blessed words, "Where sin abounded, grace did much more abound" (Rom. 5:20). We have found that the new sins of each hour, so far from closing the fountain of grace against us, opened new springs of grace for us—springs of grace which we should never otherwise have known, nor thought it possible to exist. Not as if sin were less vile on this account. David's horrid sins were the occasions of opening up new depths of grace, unimagined before; yet his iniquity lost none of its hatefulness thereby. So grace is ever gushing forth upon us to sweep away each new sin, yet in doing so it makes the sin thus swept away to appear more hideous and inexcusable. The brighter the sun, the darker and sharper are the shadows, so the fuller the grace, the viler the sin appears.

And as our personal history, as saved men, is the history of abounding sin met by more abounding grace, so is the history at large of all things in this fallen world. What is all Israel's history, every step of it, but the history of man's boundless sin drawing out the more boundless grace of God? What is the church's history but the same, so that each of the chosen and called ones who make up its mighty multitude, can say with him of old, whose name was *chief of sinners*, "The *grace* of our Lord was exceeding abundant with faith and love which is in Christ Jesus" (1 Tim. 1:14). And what is even the history of this material creation, on which the curse has pressed so long and heavily, but the history of grace abounding over sin and rescuing from the devouring fire this polluted soil?

All has been of *grace* hitherto. And all shall be of grace hereafter. In this respect there shall be no change.

Yet this is not the *whole* truth. For the brightest disclosures are yet to come. The first coming of the Lord opened up to us heights and depths of most wondrous grace, but His second coming is to bring with it discoveries of grace as marvelous, and as yet unrevealed. That promise, "The Lord will give grace and glory" (Ps. 84:11) seems specially to refer to the time, when, after days of sad longing (verse 2), and weary journeying through the valley of Baca (verse 6), we appear in Zion before God, and standing with the New Jerusalem we sing the song of blessed contrast, "A day in thy courts is better than a thousand," as if this new outburst of grace, which meets us as we enter the gates of pearl, overpasses all that we had tasted before. The apostle Peter also points forward to the same period for the full display of grace, when he speaks of "the grace that is to be brought unto us at the revelation of Jesus Christ" (1 Peter 1:13); indicating this to us, that in that day, new and larger circles of grace shall open out, just as the horizon widens when the sun ascends. To this same day the prophet Zechariah points when he says, "He shall bring forth the headstone with shoutings, crying, grace, grace unto it" (Zech. 4:7). But especially is this truth taught us by the apostle Paul when he tells us, that God's object in quickening us together with Christ, in raising us up together and making us sit together in heavenly places, is, that "in the ages to come he might show the exceeding riches of his grace in his kindness towards us through Christ Jesus." Here he heaps word upon word, as if he could find none strong enough for his purpose; it is not merely grace, but it is *riches of grace*; nay, it is not this only, it is *exceeding riches of grace;* riches of grace not only excelling all other riches, but excelling all those riches of grace that have hitherto been known, as if past grace were to be forgotten in the plenteousness of that which is to come.

How often in Israel's past days, when sin abounded, has grace come pouring in, obliterating it all as if it had never been! But in the day when "the Redeemer shall come to Zion and turn away ungodliness from Jacob," at the moment when their cry of despair may be, "Hath God forgotten to be *gracious*?" shall grace come in upon them like a flood, fuller and richer than anything that they or their fathers knew, bearing down mightier obstacles, and leveling higher mountains of iniquity. For it is written, in reference to this time, "Therefore will the Lord wait, that he may be *gracious* to *you*...he will be *very gracious* to thee at the voice of thy cry" (Isa. 30:18, 19). In that day shall "grace" not merely bring forgiveness to Israel, but raise her to a height of glory in the earth and eminence among the nations; so that the past shall not be remembered nor come into mind.

How often in the *church's* past history has grace been magnified! Each age has brought out to view new wonders of grace, because of which she has praised the God of all grace. But the abundance of the past is not all that is in store for her. Her returning Lord shall bring with him all the "exceeding riches of his grace," and upon her shall these riches be expended. When caught up into the clouds to meet her Lord in the air and to be forever with Him, she shall be led into the treasure-house of grace and get a glimpse of its vastness. Each step in her past course has drawn forth a fresh outflow of abounding grace. Grace found her in the desert land and in the waste howling wilderness. Grace drew her out of the horrible pit and out of the miry clay. Grace washed her, and "clothed" her, and "shod" her, and "girded" her, and "decked her with ornaments" (Ezek. 16:9–11), giving her beauty for ashes, the oil of joy for mourning, the garments of praise for the spirit of heaviness. Grace strengthened her for warfare, and hardship, and labor, making her more than conqueror through Him that loved her. Grace comforted her in the evil day, wiped away tears, poured in fresh joys, and threw round her the everlasting arms. Grace taught her to pray, and praise, and love, and trust, and serve, in spite of the ever-revolting heart within. Grace kept her as a stranger and a pilgrim here, without a city and without a resting-place on earth, looking for the city of foundations, watching for her Lord's appearing, amid all the heart-sickenings of hope deferred, and wearying for the Bridegroom's embrace, undazzled and undistracted by the false splendor of a present evil world. But the grace that has brought her thus far is not exhausted. For it is absolutely boundless, like the heart of Him out of whom it comes; and as it raises the church from one level to another, its own circle is ever enlarging.

The resurrection-dawn, the morning of joy, brings with it new stores of grace. We had thought that grace could go no further than it had gone here, in forgiving so many sins, in saving us with so complete a salvation; but we then shall find that grace had only begun to display itself.

It was but the first draught from the deep well that we tasted here. Grace meets us as we come up from the tomb to load us with new blessings, such as eye hath not seen nor ear heard. It clothes us with the royal raiment. It seats us upon the throne. It gives us the "crown of life" (Rev. 2:10); the "crown of righteousness" (2 Tim. 4:8). It makes us pillars in the temple of our God. It writes upon us the name of our God, and the name of the city of our God. It gives us "the morning-star." It gives us the white stone, and in the stone a new name written which no man knoweth, saving he that receiveth it. It makes us to eat of the hidden manna. It leads us back to the tree of life which is in the midst of the paradise of God. It brings us into the bridal chamber; it sets us down at the marriage table, teaching us to sing, "Let us be glad and rejoice, and give honour to him, for the marriage of the Lamb is come, and his wife hath made herself ready." It carries us into the midst of that city which has no need of the sun, neither of the moon to shine in it; whose wall is of jasper, whose foundations gems, whose gates pearls, whose streets translucent gold. It gives us to drink of the pure river of the water of life, clear as crystal, proceeding out of the throne of God and of the Lamb.

All these things grace is yet to do for us in that morning which is to dawn when this night of weeping is at an end. All this glory—this exceeding and eternal weight of glory—we shall owe to the exceeding riches of that grace which is then so marvelously to unfold itself, heaping honor upon honor, and gift upon gift, and joy upon joy, without end for ever.

In this let us mark the difference between Christ and His church, the Bridegroom and the bride. The same glory invests both; but the way of receiving it is widely different. To Him it is a reward of *righteousness,* to her of *grace.* Righteousness crowns Him, grace crowns her. These marvelous honors are in His case the claim of righteousness, in hers the mere award of grace. Of Him it is written, "Thou hast loved righteousness and hated iniquity, therefore God, even thy God, hath anointed thee with the oil of gladness above thy fellows" (Ps. 45:7); while of her it is said, "Who hath saved us and called us with an holy calling, not according to our works, but according to his own purpose and grace, which was given us in Christ Jesus before the world began" (2 Tim. 1:9). What righteousness does for Him, grace does for her.

And oh how boundless must that grace be, when it can do for her all that righteousness can do for Him!

That coming day of grace sheds light upon the present, by showing us how vast and inexhaustible that grace is which is pouring itself out from the bosom of the Father through the blood of the Son. If these riches of grace be so exceeding great, then how is it possible for us to entertain the suspicion that so often haunts us now, "Is there grace enough for the pardon of sins like mine, grace enough to secure welcome and acceptance to a sinner like me?" What, is there grace enough to receive myriads, washing them clean and presenting them blameless in the day of the Lord with exceeding joy, and is there not enough for *one*? Is there grace enough to pour out such wondrous glory upon the multitudes of the undeserving hereafter, and is there not enough to bring forgiveness to one undeserving soul just now? So that in thus telling of the grace which the ages to come are to unroll, we are proclaiming *good news* to the chief of sinners— good news concerning the infinite largeness of grace, good news concerning Him out of whom this blessed stream is flowing. Oh, what a rebuke to fear, to doubt, to suspicion, to unbelief, is the truth concerning these exceeding riches of grace yet to be developed! Is it possible that we can go on, fearing, doubting, suspecting, misbelieving, with the assured knowledge that grace is so free and large, so sufficient to embrace the whole circumstances of our case, so suitable to each special want, each special burden, each special sin? Shall we dare to make more of the sin than of the grace, of the want than of the supply, of the burden than of the relief? Shall we not be ashamed to magnify our *sin* beyond the *grace of God,* and to reason as if the grace that can confer on us the kingdom and the crown of Christ were not large enough in compass to cover our sins? Oh the folly of unbelief—folly without a name and without an equal, to believe in a grace willing to place us on the throne of the universe by the side of the everlasting Son, yet not willing to pardon us! A grace large enough to say, "Come, ye blessed of my Father, inherit the kingdom prepared for you before the foundation of the world," yet not large enough to say, "Be of good cheer, thy sins are forgiven thee!"

"It doth not indeed yet appear what we shall be." Yet, as the womb of grace knows no abortions, we know "that he who has begun the good work in us will perform it until the day of Jesus Christ." The grace has not had full room to expand itself and show all the vastness of its compass. Our life is hid; our glory is hid; our inheritance is hid, our city has not yet come down out of heaven from God. In the pit of Dothan it did not appear what Joseph was to be. His strange dreams did betoken something, yet who could have thought that he was to sit upon Pharaoh's throne? It did not appear what Ruth was to be when she lived in Moab, a stranger to the true God, or even when she left home and kindred to cast in her lot with Israel. That blessed scene of love and faith when "Orpah kissed" and "Ruth clave," giving forth a heart of no common mold, did intimate something, but who could have thought that she was to be a mother in Israel, from whom Messiah was to spring?

So we do not now wear the aspect of that which we shall be. We do not look like kings. And though at times, when we get a glimpse of the promised crown, and when a vision of its nearness passes before us, our face flushes, our eye kindles, our gait unconsciously assumes unusual dignity, yet in general we look very unlike that which we shall be. Sometimes the star of nobility—the badge of our order—flashes out from the sordid covering and glitters on our breast, yet this is seldom; more seldom now in these last days than formerly. For religion, even the best, has sunk down from its primitive loftiness into a tame, second-rate, inferior thing, and the still-clinging garments of the old man cover in or quench every rising ray of anticipated glory.

What different beings grace would make us would we but allow it! Yet, instead of allowing it, we put it from us, content with just as much of it as will save us from the wrath to come. We shrink from its fullness, as if we should thereby stand committed to a far holier walk and higher style of living than we are prepared for. For "the grace of God that bringeth salvation teacheth us to deny ungodliness and worldly lusts, and to live soberly, righteously, and godly in this present world, looking for that blessed hope, even the glorious appearing of the great God, and our Saviour Jesus Christ, who gave himself for us that he might redeem us from all iniquity, and purify unto himself a peculiar people zealous of good works."

The grace that flowed in upon us during our long night has been large and manifold; but it is not ended with the night. The morning brings with it new stores of grace. When that grace unfolds itself, then shall it appear what we really are. Our present guise will fall from us, we shall stand forth as "heirs of God," and He who hath given us grace shall also give us glory; He who led us through the night shall bring us forth to the joy of the morning.

12

The Glory

Not only a man's true *life,* but a man's true *history* begins with his conversion. Up until that time, he is a being without a history. He has no story to tell. He is but part of a world lying in wickedness, having nothing about him worthy of a record.

But from the moment that he is born again, and thus taken out of the mass, he receives a *personality* as well as a dignity which fit him for having a history—a history which God can own as such, and which God Himself will record. From that time he has a story to tell, wondrous and divine, such as angels listen to, and over which there is joy in heaven.

In that broad ocean, there are millions of drops; yet they are one mingled mass of fluid; no one of them has a history. There may be a history of the ocean, but not of its individual drops. But, see, your drop is beginning to part from the mass. It takes hold of a sunbeam and rises into the firmament. There it gleams in the rainbow or brightens in the hues of sunset. It has now a history. From the moment that it came out of the mass and obtained a personality, it had a story to tell, a story of its own, a story of splendor and beauty.

In those vast blocks of unquarried rock what various forms are lying concealed! What shapes of statuary or architecture are there! Yet they have no history. They can have none. They are but parts of a hideous block, in which not one line or curve of beauty is visible. But the noise of hammers is heard. Man lifts up his tool. A single block is severed. Again he lifts up his tool, and it begins to assume a form; till, as stroke after stroke falls on it, and touch after touch smooths and shapes it, the perfect image of the human form is seen, and it seems as if the hand of the artist had only been employed in unwrapping the stony folds from that fair form, and awakening it from the slumber of its marble tomb. From the moment that the chisel touched that piece of rock its history began.

Such is the case of a saint. From the moment that the hand of the Spirit is laid on him to begin the process of separation, from that moment his history begins. He then receives a conscious, outstanding personality, that fits him for having a history—a history entirely marvelous; a history whose pages are both written and read in heaven; a history which in its divine brightness spreads over eternity. His true dignity now commences. He is fit to take a place in history. Each event in his life becomes worthy of a record. "The righteous shall be in everlasting remembrance."

On earth this history is one of suffering and dishonor, even as was that of the Master; but hereafter, in the kingdom, it is one of glory and honor. "All the time," says Howe, "from the soul's first conversion, God has been at work upon it, laboring, shaping it, polishing it, spreading His own glory on it, inlaying, enamelling it with glory; now at last the whole work is revealed, the curtain is drawn aside, and the blessed soul awakes." Then a new epoch in its history begins.

What that history is to be, we know not now. That it will be wondrous, we know; how wondrous we cannot conceive. That it will be very unlike our present one, we know; yet still not severed from it, but linked to it, nay, springing out of it as its root or seed. Our present life is the *under-ground* state of the plant; our future life, the shooting, and blossoming, and fruitbearing; but the plant is the same, and the future depends for all its excellency and beauty upon the present.

Night is not the shutting up of day, but day is the opening out of night. Day is but the night in blossom, the expanded petals of some dark, unsightly bud, containing within it glories of which no glimpses have yet reached us here. It is moody sentiment, as well as false philosophy, to say as one in our day has done, "Night is nobler than day; day is but a motley-colored veil, spread transiently over the infinite bosom of night, hiding from us its purely transparent, eternal deeps." Night is at best but the beauty of death; day, of life. And it is life, not death, that is beautiful. And if life on earth, in all its various forms and unfoldings, be so very beautiful, what will it not be hereafter, when it unfolds itself to the full, transfused throughout all being, with an intensity now unknown, as if almost becoming visible by means of the new glory which it then shall spread over all creation.

"The wise shall inherit *glory*" (Prov. 3:35). "The saints shall be joyful in *glory*" (Ps. 149:5). They are "vessels of mercy, afore prepared unto *glory*" (Rom. 9:23). That to which we are called is "eternal *glory*" (1 Peter 5:10). That which we obtain is "salvation in Christ Jesus with *eternal glory*" (2 Tim. 2:10). It is to *glory* that God is "bringing many sons" (Heb. 2:10); so that as He, through whom we are brought to it, is "crowned with *glory* and honour," so shall we be (Heb. 2:9). We are "to rejoice with joy unspeakable and full of *glory*" (1 Peter 1:8). We are not only "witnesses of the sufferings of Christ, but partakers of the *glory* that shall be revealed" (1 Peter 5:1). So that the word of exhortation runs thus: "Rejoice, inasmuch as ye are partakers of Christ's sufferings; that when his *glory* shall be revealed, ye may be glad also with exceeding joy" (1 Peter 4:13). And the promise is not only, "if we suffer we shall also reign with him;" but, "if we suffer with him, we shall be also *glorified* together" (Rom. 8:17).

This glory, then, is our portion. It is the "better thing" that God has provided for us, and because of which he is not ashamed to be called our God. This is the glory that throws all present suffering into the shade, making it to be eternally forgotten.

Glory is the concentrated essence of all that is holy, excellent, and beautiful. For all being has its more and its less perfect parts. And its glory is that which is most perfect about it, to which of course that which is less perfect has, according to its measure, contributed. Light is the glory of the sun. Transparency is the glory of the stream. The flower is the glory of the plant. The soul is the glory of the man. The face is the glory of the body. And this glory is strangely manifold: "There is one glory of the sun, and another glory of the moon, and another glory of the stars, for star differeth from star in glory."

What is really glorious is so hidden, so blighted, so intermixed with deformity and corruption here, that Scripture always speaks as if the whole glory were yet in reserve, none of it yet revealed. So that when *He* came to earth who was "the brightness of Jehovah's glory," He was not recognized as the possessor of such glory; it was hidden; it shone not. Few eyes saw *any* glory at all in Him; none saw the extent or greatness of it. Even in *His* case it did not appear what He was and what He shall be, when He comes "to be *glorified* in his saints."

All that is glorious, whether visible or invisible, material or immaterial, natural or spiritual, must have its birth-place in God. "Of him, and through him, and to him are all things, to whom be glory for ever" (Rom. 11:36). All glorious things come forth out of Him, and have their seeds, or gems, or patterns in Him. We say of that flower, "how beautiful"; but the type of its beauty—the beauty of which it is the faint expression—is in God. We say of the star, "how bright"; but the brightness which it represents or declares, is in God. So of every object above and beneath. And so especially shall it be seen in the objects of glory which shall surround us in the kingdom of God. Of each thing there, as of the city itself, it shall be said, "it has the glory of God" (Rev. 21:11).

Glory, then, is our inheritance. The best, the richest, the brightest, the most beautiful of all that is in God, of good, and rich, and bright, and beautiful, shall be ours. The glory that fills heaven above, the glory that spreads over the earth beneath, shall be ours. But while "the glory of the *terrestrial*" shall be ours, yet in a truer sense "the glory of the *celestial* shall be ours." Already by faith we have taken our place amid things celestial, "being quickened together with Christ, and raised up with him, and made to sit with him in *heavenly* places" (Eph. 2:6). Thus we have already claimed *the celestial* as our own; and having risen with Christ, we "set our affection upon things *above,* not on things *on the earth*" (Col. 3:2). Far-ranging dominion shall be ours; with all varying shades and kinds of glory shall we be encompassed, circle beyond circle stretching over the universe; but it is the *celestial* glory that is so truly ours, as the redeemed and the risen; and in the midst of that celestial glory shall be the family mansion, the church's dwelling-place and palace—our true home for eternity.

All that awaits us is glorious. There is an inheritance in reversion; and it is "an inheritance incorruptible, and undefiled, and that fadeth not away" (1 Peter 1:4). There is a rest, a sabbath-keeping in store for us (Heb. 4:9); and this "rest shall be glorious" (Isa. 11:10). The kingdom which we claim is a glorious kingdom. The crown which we are to wear is a glorious crown. The city of our habitation is a glorious city. The garments which shall clothe us are garments "for glory and for beauty." Our bodies shall be glorious bodies, fashioned after the likeness of Christ's "glorious body" (Phil. 3:21). Our society shall be that of the glorified. Our songs shall be songs of glory. And of the region which we are to inhabit it is said, that "the glory of God doth lighten it, and the Lamb is the light thereof" (Rev. 21:23).

The hope of this glory cheers us. From under a canopy of night we look out upon these promised scenes of blessedness, and we are comforted. Our dark thoughts are softened down, even when they are not wholly brightened. For day is near, and joy is near, and the warfare is ending, and the tear shall be dried up, and the shame be lost in the glory, and "we shall be presented faultless before the presence of his glory with exceeding joy."

Then the fruit of patience and of faith shall appear, and the hope we have so long been clinging to shall not put us to shame. Then shall we triumph and praise. Then shall we be avenged on death, and pain, and sickness. Then shall every wound be more than healed. Egypt enslaves us no more. Babylon leads us captive no more. The Red Sea is crossed, the wilderness is passed, Jordan lies behind us, and we are in Jerusalem! There is no more curse—there is no more night. The tabernacle of God is with us; in that tabernacle He dwells, and we dwell with Him.

It is "the God of all grace" who "has called us to his eternal *glory* by Christ Jesus." It is "when the chief Shepherd shall appear, that we shall receive the crown of *glory* that fadeth not away" (1 Peter 5:4, 10). And this "after we have suffered a while," and by suffering have been "made perfect, stablished, strengthened, settled." So that suffering is not lost upon us. It prepares us for the glory. And the hope of that glory, as well as the knowledge of the discipline through which we are passing, and of the process of preparation going on in us, sustains us, nay, teaches us to "glory in tribulation." This comfort, nay, it is happiness. Strange in the world's eye, but not strange in ours! All that the world has is but a poor imitation of happiness and consolation; ours is real, even now; how much more hereafter! Nor will a brief delay and a sore conflict lessen the weight of coming glory. Nay, they will add to it; and it is worth waiting for, it is worth suffering for, it is worth fighting for. It is so sure of coming, and so blessed when it comes.

"The mass of glory," says Howe, "is yet in reserve; we are not yet so high as the highest heavens." All this is hanging over us, inviting us on, stirring us up, loosening us from things present, so that the pain of loss, or sickness, or bereavement, falls more gently on us, and tends but to make us less vain and light, more thoroughly in earnest.

"That they may behold my glory," the Lord pleaded for His own. This is the sum of all. Other glories there will be, as we have seen; but this is the sum of all. It is the very utmost that even "the Lord of glory" could ask for them. Having sought this He could seek no more; He could go no further. And our response to this is, "Let me see thy glory;" yes, and the glad confidence in which we rest is this, "As for me, I will behold thy face in righteousness; I shall be satisfied, when I awake, with thy likeness." This is our ambition. Divine and blessed ambition, in which there is no pride, no presumption, and no excess! Nothing less can satisfy than the directest, fullest vision of incarnate glory. Self-emptied before the Infinite Majesty, and conscious of being wholly unworthy even of a servant's place, we yet feel as if drawn irresistibly into the innermost circle and center, satisfied with nothing less than the fullness of Him that filleth all in all.

"The glory that thou gavest me I have given them" (John 17:22). No less than this, both in kind and amount, is the glory in reserve, according to the promise of the Lord. The glory given to Him He makes over to them! They "are made partakers of Christ," and all that he has is theirs. Nay, and He says, "I *have* given"; as if it were already theirs by His gift, just as truly as it was His by the Father's gift. He receives it from the Father only for the purpose of immediately handing it over to them! So that even here they can say, "This glory is already mine, and I must live as one to whom such infinite glory belongs." "Beholding, as in a glass, this glory of the

Lord, they are changed into the same image from glory to glory" (2 Cor. 3:18). To fret or despond is sad inconsistency in one who can say, even under sorest pressures, "I reckon that the sufferings of this present time are not worthy to be compared with the glory that shall be revealed in us." Look at them by themselves, and they do seem at times most overwhelming; place them side by side with the eternal glory, and they disappear.

"The riches of his glory," says the apostle in one place (Rom. 9:23); "the riches of the glory of his inheritance in the saints," writes he in another (Eph. 1:18). Strange expressions these! They carry us up to a height of such infinite glory and joy, that we feel bewildered and overwhelmed. Just as there are "riches of grace," and "riches of mercy," and "riches of love," and "riches of wisdom," so there are "riches of glory"; glory in abundance, such as shall make us rich indeed; glory spreads over our whole inheritance, so that we shall "have all and abound." Nay, this glory is that which God counts His riches, that which He reckons the perfection of His inheritance, the very essence of its beauty and its blessedness.

"The liberty of the *glory* of the children of God," writes the apostle (Rom. 8:21), thereby telling us that there is a glory which is the peculiar property of the saints—a glory of which they can say, it is our own, thereby marking it out from the glory of all other creatures. This glory contains *liberty*. It sets free those who possess it. Corruption had brought with it chains and bondage; glory brings with it divine liberty! It is not the liberty that brings the glory; it is the glory that brings the liberty. Blessed liberty! Freedom from every bondage! Not only the bondage of corruption and sin and death, but the bondage of *sorrow*! For is not sorrow a bondage? Are not it chains sharp and heavy? From this bondage of tribulation the glory sets us eternally free. It is the last fetter, save that of the grave, that is struck from our bruised limbs, but when it is broken, it is broken for ever!

And this liberty which the glory brings to us is one which shall extend to the unconscious creation around us. We brought that creation into bondage, covering it with dishonor, and making it the prey of corruption. It now groans and travails under this sore bondage. But as it has shared our bondage, it is also to share our liberty; and that same glory which brings liberty to us shall introduce the oppressed and dishonored creation into the same blessed freedom! O longed-for consummation! O joyful hope! O welcome day, when the Bringer of this glory shall arrive, and the voice be heard from heaven, "Behold, I make all things new."

Nor is it liberty only which this glory contains in it, but power also, as it is written, "strengthened with all might according to the power of his glory" (Col. 1:11). This glory has, even now, a power-giving energy, whereby we are strengthened "to all patience and longsuffering with joyfulness." Thus "rejoicing in hope of the glory of God" (Rom. 5:2), we are fitted for all manner of tribulation and endurance. Though still among the things "not seen," it not only flings forward a radiance which brightens our path, but sheds down a strength which enables us to "run with patience the race that is set before us." And so, in an unholy world, we "walk worthy of him who hath called us unto his kingdom and glory" (1 Thess. 2:12), having that prayer fulfilled in us, "The God of all grace, who hath called us unto his eternal *glory* by Jesus Christ, after that ye have suffered a while, make you perfect, stablish, strengthen, settle you" (1 Peter 5:10).

"Christ in you the hope of *glory*." An indwelling Christ is our earnest, our pledge, our hope of glory. Having Him, we have all that is His, whether present or to come. He is the link that binds together the *here* and the *hereafter.* We died with Him, we went down into the tomb with Him, we rose with Him, and our life is now hid with Him in God; but "when Christ, who is our life, shall appear, then shall we also appear with him in glory" (Col. 3:4).

The joy with which we rejoice is a joy "unspeakable and full of glory," or more literally, a "glorified joy"; a joy such as Paul had when caught up into paradise; a joy such as John's when placed in vision within sight of the celestial city; a joy into whose very essence the thoughts of glory enter; a joy which makes the soul which possesses it feel as if it were already compassed about with glory, as if it had "come to Mount Zion, to the city of the living God, the heavenly Jerusalem, to an innumerable company of angels, to the general assembly and church of the first-born which are written in heaven" (Heb. 12:22).

"The glorious gospel of Christ," says the apostle (2 Cor. 4:4); and again, "the glorious gospel of the blessed God" (1 Tim. 1:11); or, more literally, "the gospel of the glory of Christ," that is, "the good news about the *glory* of Christ," and "the good news about the glory of the blessed God." As it is "the gospel of the kingdom," or good news about "the kingdom," that is preached, so it is good news about "the glory." This good news God has sent, and is still sending to this world. In believing it, and receiving God's record concerning the glory, we become partakers of it, and continue to be so, "if we hold the beginning of our confidence stedfast unto the end." This good news most fully meets our case, however sad or sinful, and sheds light into our souls even in their darkest and most desponding hours.

Our present "light affliction, which is but for a moment, worketh for us a far more exceeding and eternal weight of *glory*." So that glory is not merely the *issue* of tribulation, but in some sense its *product*. Tribulation is the soil, and glory is the blossom and the fruit. The soil is rough and unseemly, but the produce is altogether perfect. It may seem strange that out of such a field there should spring verdure so fresh and fruit so divine. Yet we know that such is the case. How much we owe to that unlikely soil! Not only do all things work together for good to us, but they as truly work together for *glory.*

Faith lays hold of this and *prizes* tribulation, nay, glories in it; so realizing the joy as to lose sight of the sorrow, save as contributing to the joy; so absorbed in the glory as to forget the shame, excepting in so far as it is the parent and precursor of the glory.

Most needful is it that we should realize these prospects, these glimpses which God has given us of what we are yet to be. It is not merely lawful to do so for the relief of the laden spirit, but it is most vitally important to do so for the *health* of our soul, for our growth in grace, and for enabling us to press on with cheerful energy in the path of service towards God and usefulness to our brother saints or fellow men.

The man of sorrows had joy set before Him. And it was for this that He endured the cross, despising the shame (Heb. 12:2). He needed it, and so do we; for He who sanctifieth and they who are sanctified are all of one. He found in it strength for the bearing of the cross and the endurance of the shame. So may we, for as the path He trod is the same that is given us to tread in, so the strength is to be found where our Forerunner found it. There is joy in store for us, even as for Him; joy not only like His own, but His own very joy (John 11). This makes us willing to bear the cross in all its weight and sharpness; nay, it lightens it so that ofttimes we do not feel its pressure. We can glory both in the cross and the shame. We have less of these than He had, and we have all His consolation, all His joy to the full.

When this is lost sight of, selfish melancholy often fastens on us. We brood over our griefs till they engross us entirely, to the shutting out of all else. We magnify them; we spread them out and turn them over on every side in order to find out the gloomiest. We take credit to ourselves for endurance, and thus feed our pride and self-importance. We fret under them, and at the same time grow vain at being the objects of so much sympathy—at having so many eyes upon us, and so many words of comfort addressed to us.

Nothing can be more *unhealthy* than this state of soul, not more unlike that in which God expects a saint to be. It shuts us into the narrow circle of self. It contracts as well as distorts our vision. It vitiates our spiritual tastes, it lowers our spiritual tone, it withers and shrivels up our spiritual being, unfitting us for all offices of calm and gentle love, nay, hindering the right discharge of plain and common duty. It is in itself a sore disease, and is the source of other diseases without number.

To meet this unhealthy tendency God seeks to draw us out of ourselves. He does so in holding up the *cross* for us to look upon and be healed, but He also does this by exhibiting the crown and throne. The cross does not annihilate man's natural concern for self, but it loosens our thoughts from this, by showing us, upon the cross, One to whose care we may safely entrust self with all its interests, and in whose pierced hands it will be far better provided for than in our own. So the vision of the glory does not make away with self, but it absorbs it, and elevates it, by revealing the kingdom in which God has made such blessed and enduring provision for us, as to make it appear worse than folly in us to brood over our case, and make *self* the object of our sad and anxious care. If we are to have glory as surely and as cheaply as the lilies have their clothing, or the ravens their food, why be so solicitous about self? Or why think about self at all, save to remember and to rejoice that God has taken all our concerns into His own keeping for eternity.

Thus God beguiles us away from our griefs by giving us something else to muse over—something more worthy of our thoughts. He allures us from the present, where all is dark and uncomely, into the future, where all is bright and fair. He takes us by the hand and leads us, as a father his child, out from the gloomy region which we are sadly pacing, with our eye upon the ground, bent only upon nourishing our sorrows, into fields where all is fresh and Eden-like; so that, ere we are aware, joy, or at least the faint reflection of it, has stolen into our hearts, and lifted up our heavy eyes. He would not have us abiding always in the church-yard, or sitting upon the turf beneath which love is buried, as if the tomb to which we are clinging were our hope, not resurrection beyond it. He would have us to come forth; and having allured us away from that scene of death, He bids us look upwards, upbraiding us with our unbelief and folly, and saying to us, "They whom you love are yonder; ere long He who is their life and yours shall appear, and you shall rejoin each other, each of you embracing, not a weeping, sickly fellow mortal, but a glorified saint, set free from pain and sin."

There is nothing more *healthy* and genial for the soul than these anticipations of the morning, and of morning-glory. They are not visionary, save in the sense in which faith is "the substance of things hoped for, the evidence of things not seen." They transfuse the life of heaven through our frame, either, on the one hand, making our languid pulse to beat more swiftly, or, on the other, our feverish pulse to throb more calmly and evenly. They act as regulators of the soul in its wild and inconstant movements, neither allowing us to sink too low nor to soar too high. They tend to steady our extreme impulses by acting as a counterpoise to the weight of grief which so crushes us with its pressure.

They withdraw us from self and self-broodings, they widen the circle of our sympathies, and throw back into the distance the fence of exclusiveness, which, in times of suffering, we are apt to throw up around ourselves. They check mere sentimentality, and forbid us to indulge the flow of grief for its own luxury. They prohibit morbid gloom, which loves to shun out society, and chooses loneliness. They fill us with energy for facing the toils, and with ready courage for braving the dangers of the night. They animate us with the calm but indomitable confidence of hope, a hope which expands and brightens as its object approaches.

The morning! That is our watchword. Our matin and even song are full of it. It gives the hue to life, imparting color to that which is colorless, and freshening that which is faded. It is the sum and term of our hopes. Nothing else will do for us or for our world, a world over which the darkness gathers thicker as the years run out. Stars may help to make the sky less gloomy, but they are not the sun. And besides, clouds have now wrapped them so that they are no longer visible. The firmament is almost without a star. Torches and beacon-lights avail not. They make no impression upon the darkness; it is so deep, so real, so palpable. We might give up all for lost, were we not assured that there is a sun, and that it is hastening to rise. The church's pilgrimage is nearly done. Yet she is not less a pilgrim as its end draws nigh. Nay, more so. The last stage of the journey is the dreariest for her. Her path lies through the thickest darkness that the world has yet felt. It seems as if it were only by the fitful blaze of conflagrations that we can now shape our way. It is the sound of falling kingdoms that is guiding us onward. It is the fragments of broken thrones lying across our path that assures us that our route is the true one, and that its end is near—that end, the morning with its songs; and in that morning, a kingdom; and in that kingdom, glory; and in that glory, the everlasting rest, the sabbath of eternity.